My name is

....

My teacher's name is

....

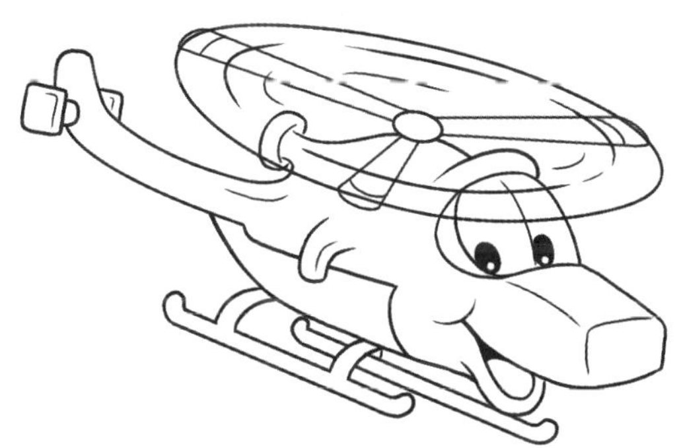

My learning goals and success criteria:

- I can trace and write all lower-case letters of the alphabet in NSW Foundation style.
- I can trace and write all capital letters of the alphabet in NSW Foundation style.
- I can trace and write all numerals 1 to 100 in NSW Foundation style.

Are you ready to write?

Posture

Is your back resting against the chair?

Are your feet flat on the floor?

Paper position

left-handed

Are you holding the paper steady with your non-writing hand?

right-handed

Pencil grip

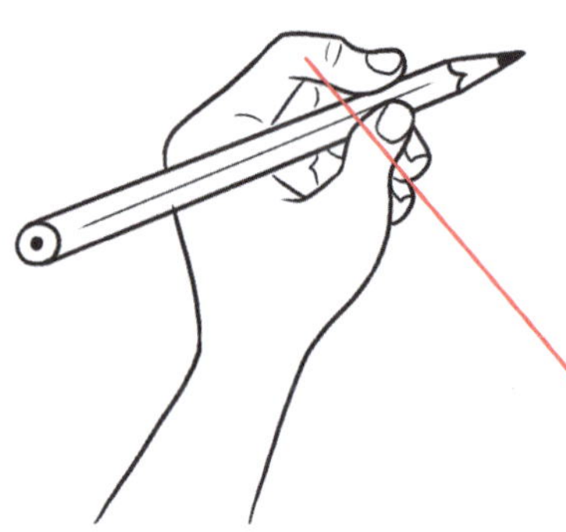

Is one finger on top of the pencil?

Left-handers, hold your pencil a little further up so you can see your handwriting!

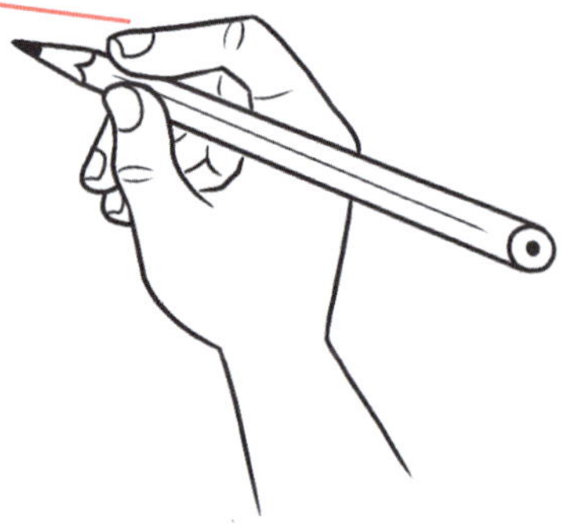

1, 2, 3, 4! Are my feet flat on the floor?
5, 6, 7, 8! Is my back up nice and straight?
9, 10, 11, 12! Show me how your pencil's held!
Thumb and pointer side-by-side, lucky tall one takes a ride!

Start at the dots. Follow the arrows.

Start at the dots. Follow the arrows.

Start at the dots. Follow the arrows.

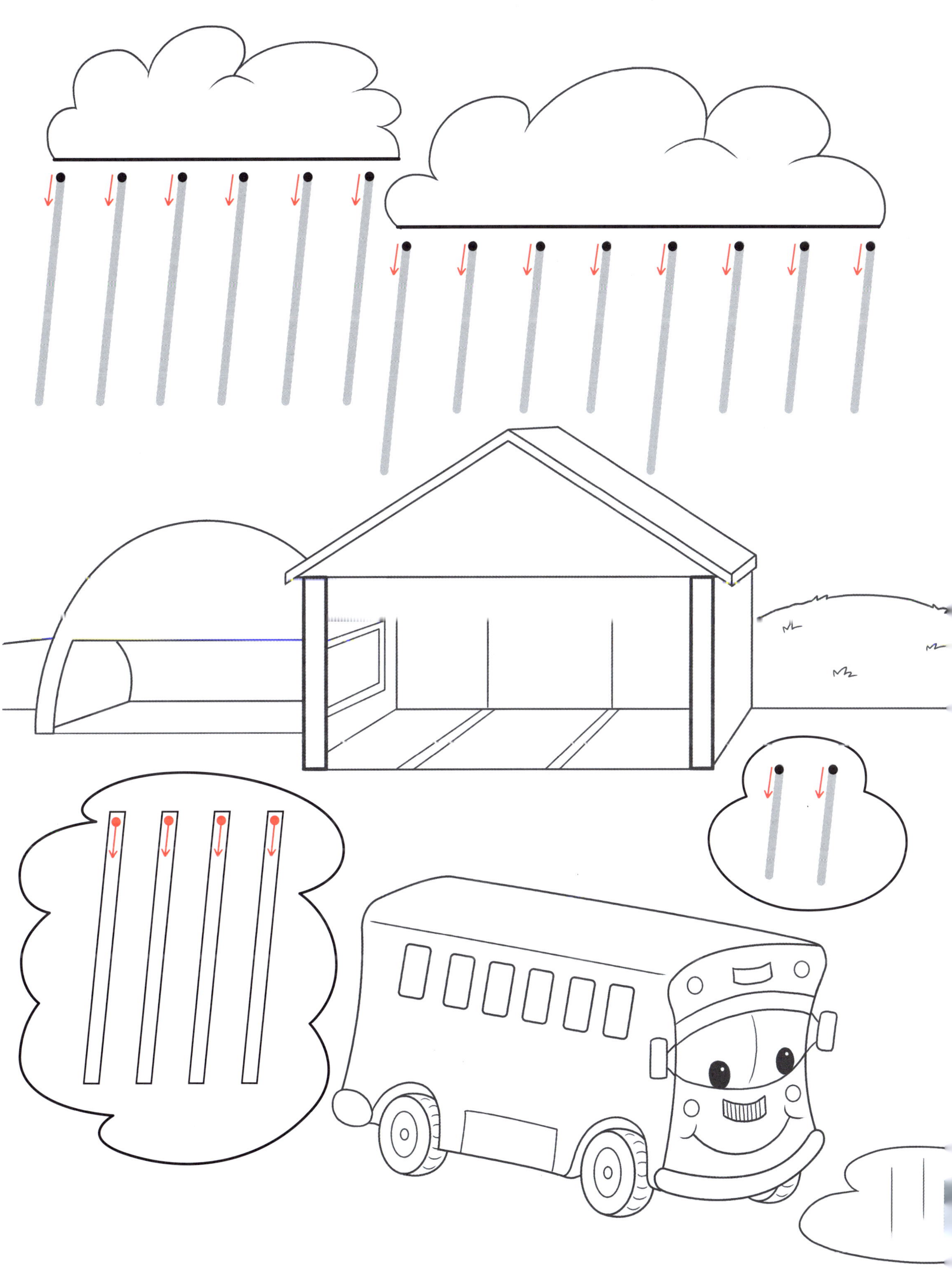

'r' is a body letter.

Trace and copy all the body letters.

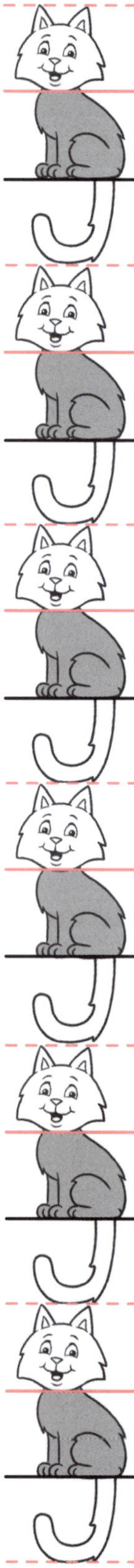

a c e i m

n o r s u

v w x z

'b' is a head and body letter.

Trace and copy all the head and body letters.

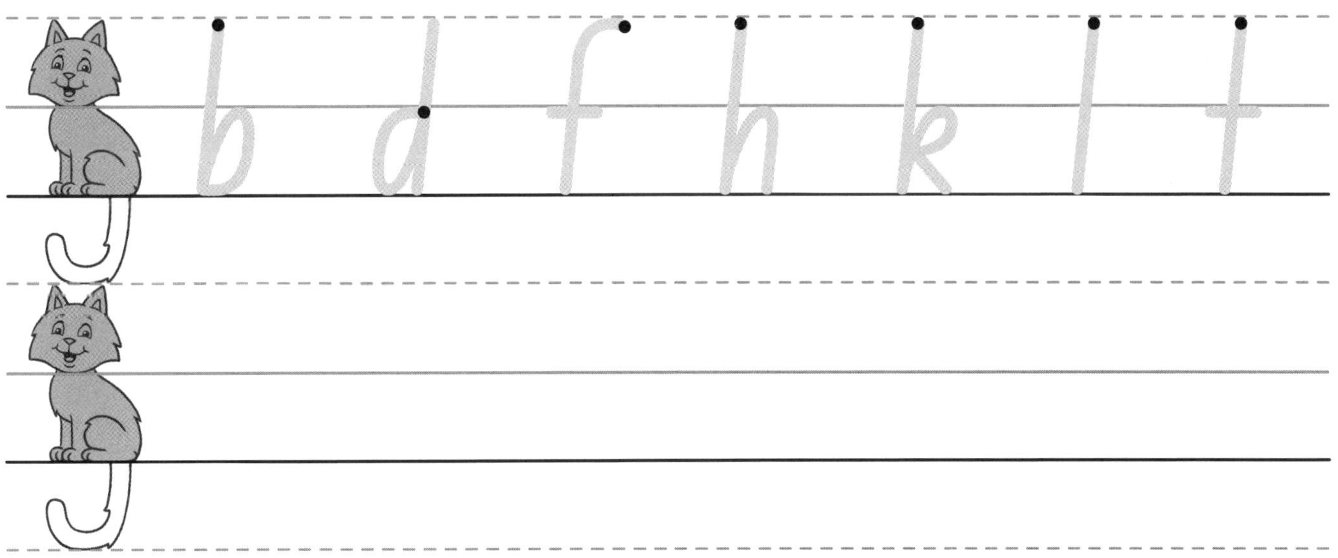

'g' is a body and tail letter.

Trace and copy all the body and tail letters.

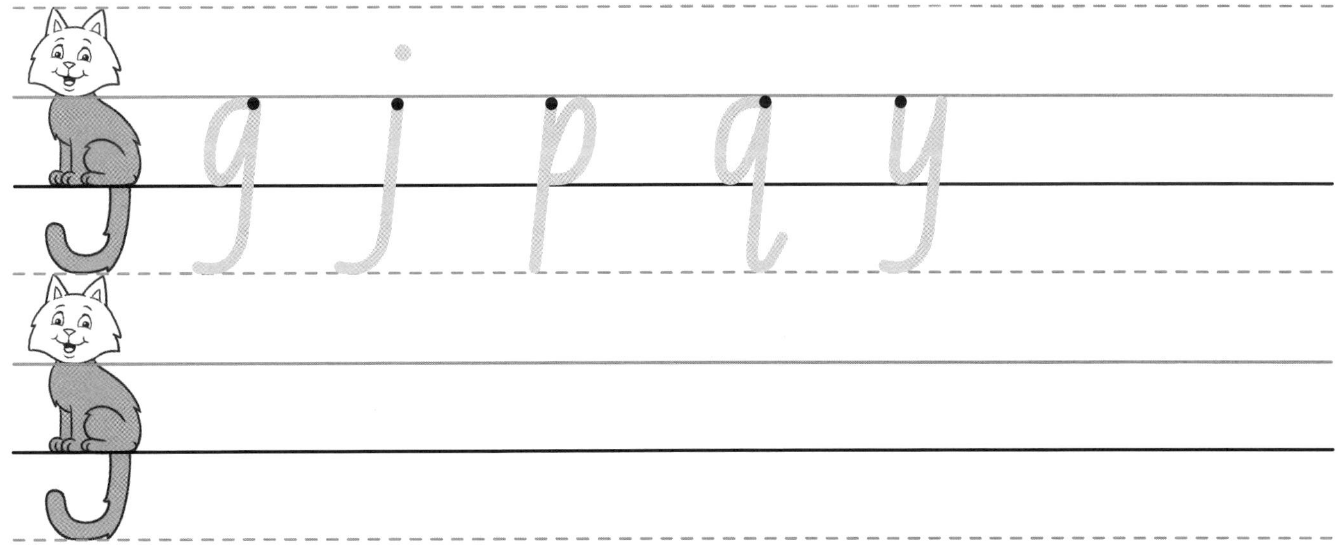

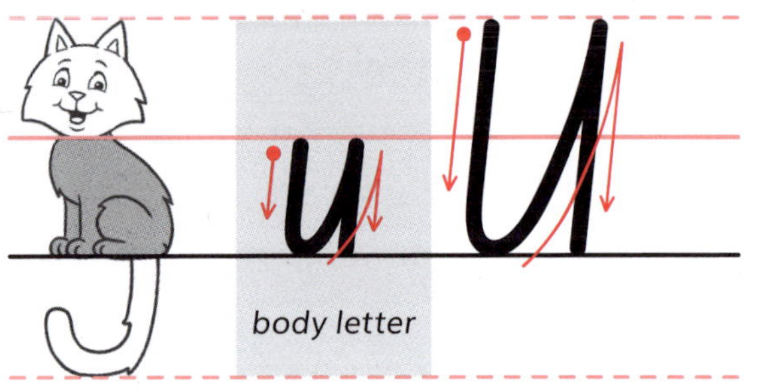

Track.

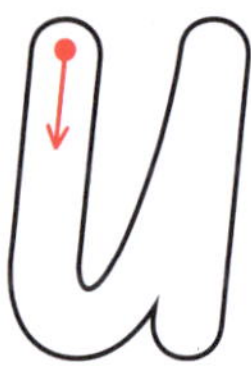
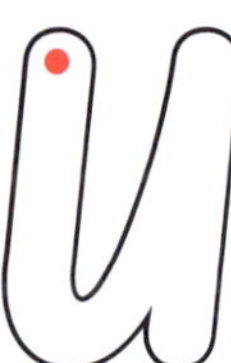

Find ‘u’ and colour the wedge.

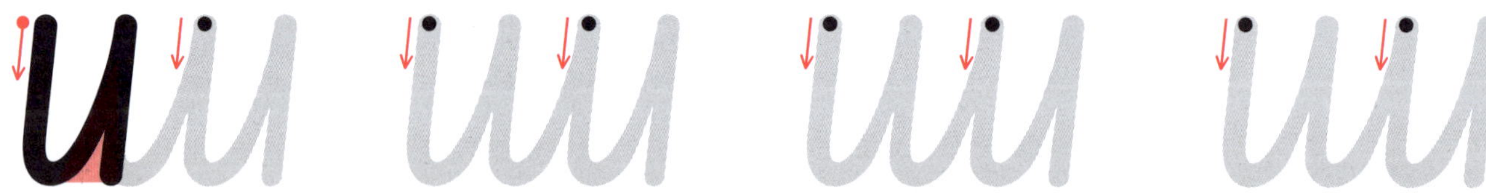

Trace and copy. Complete the lines.

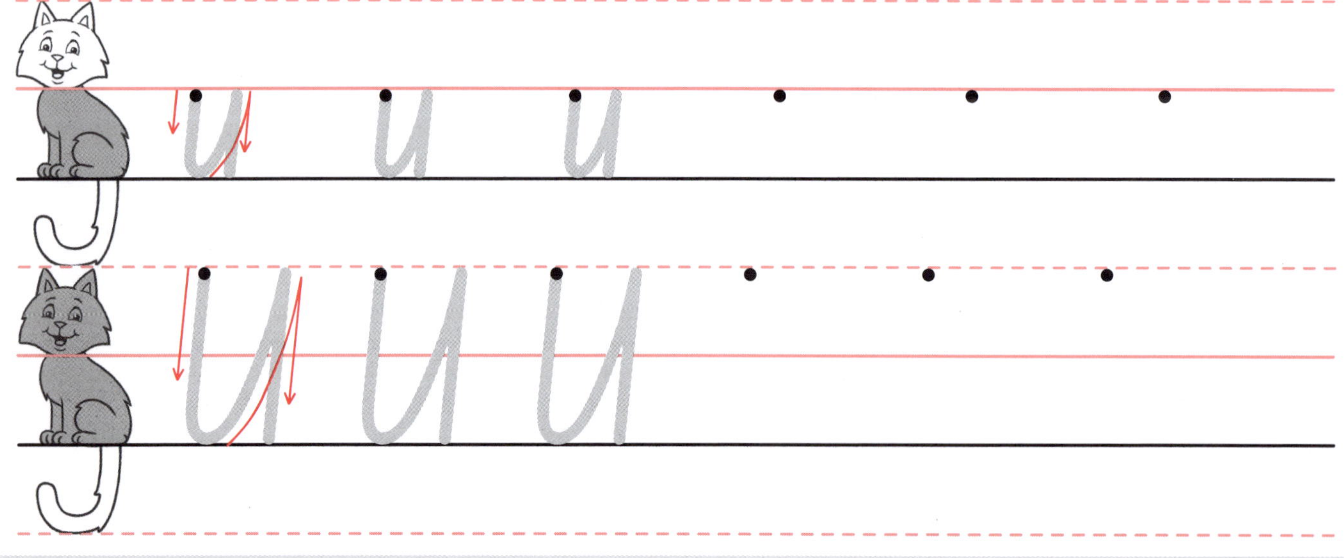

Trace and copy.

up up up up

The Toytown bus

was going up the hill.

yawn

Track.

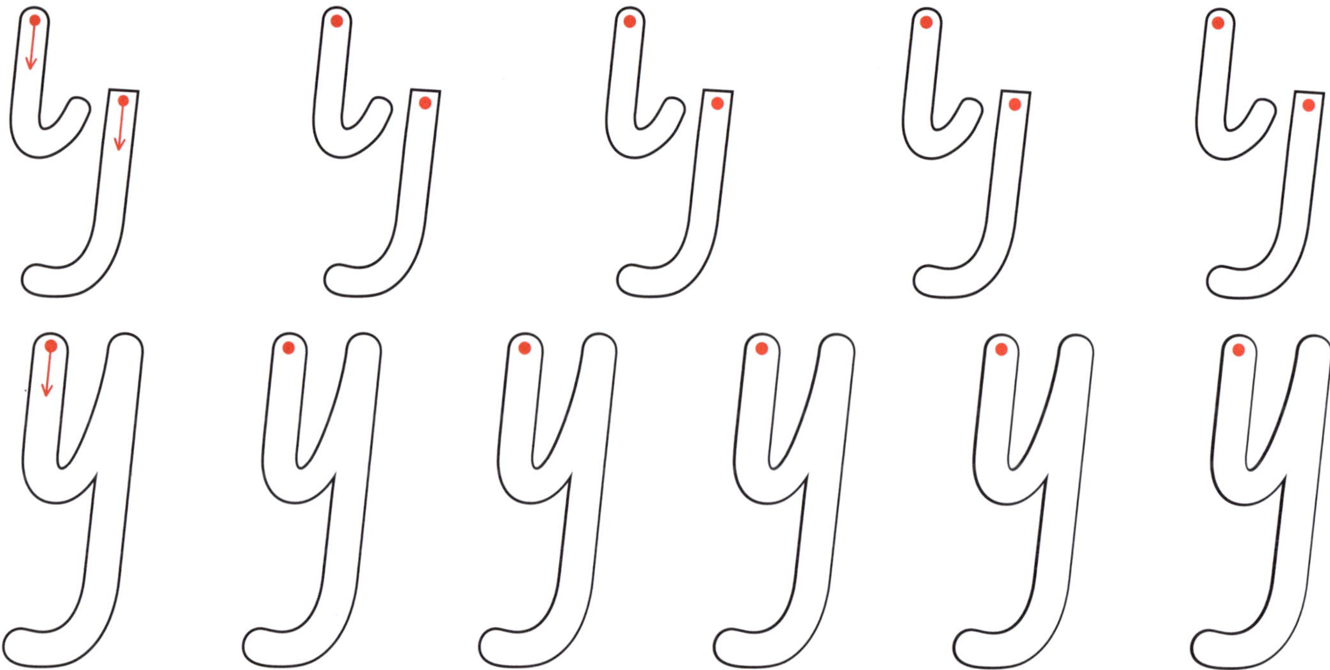

Find 'y' and colour the wedge.

Trace and copy. Complete the lines.

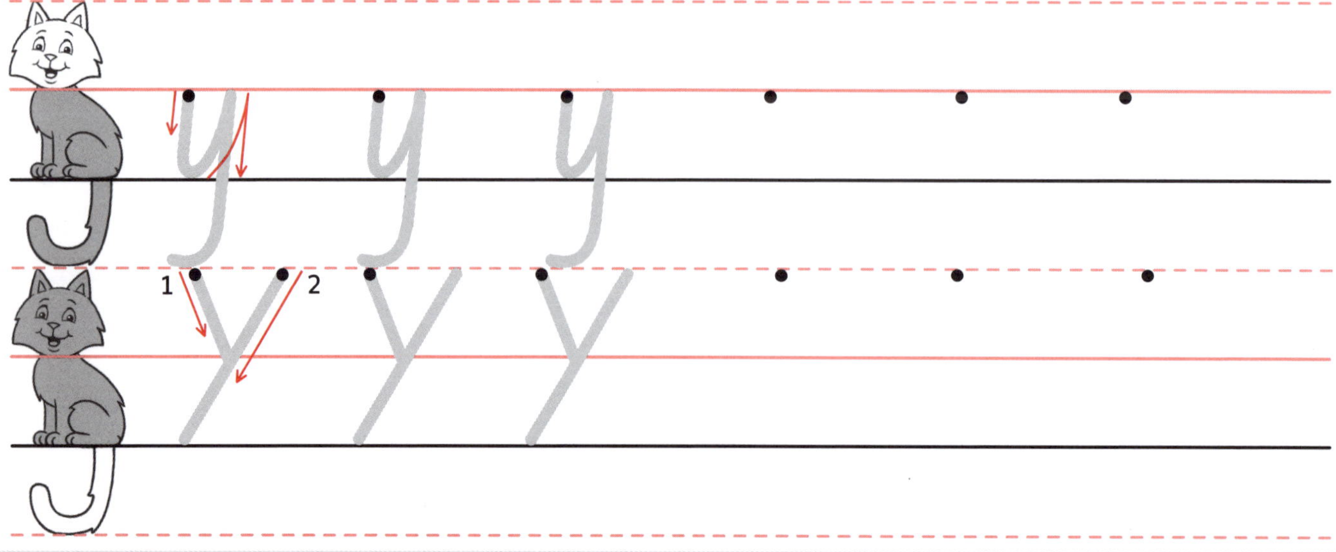

Trace and copy.

yet yet yet yet

"I am not at the top of the hill yet!"

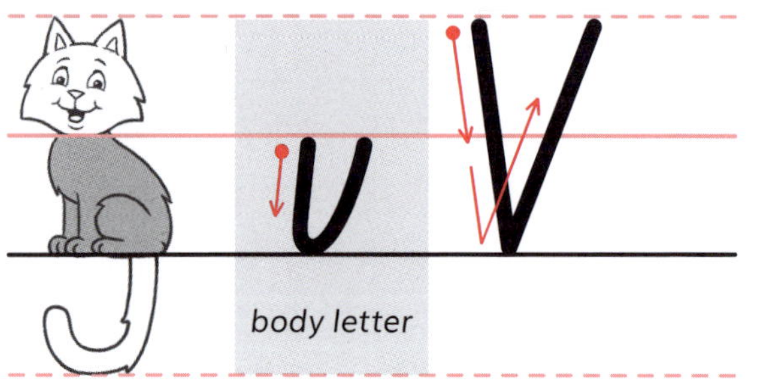

vase

Track.

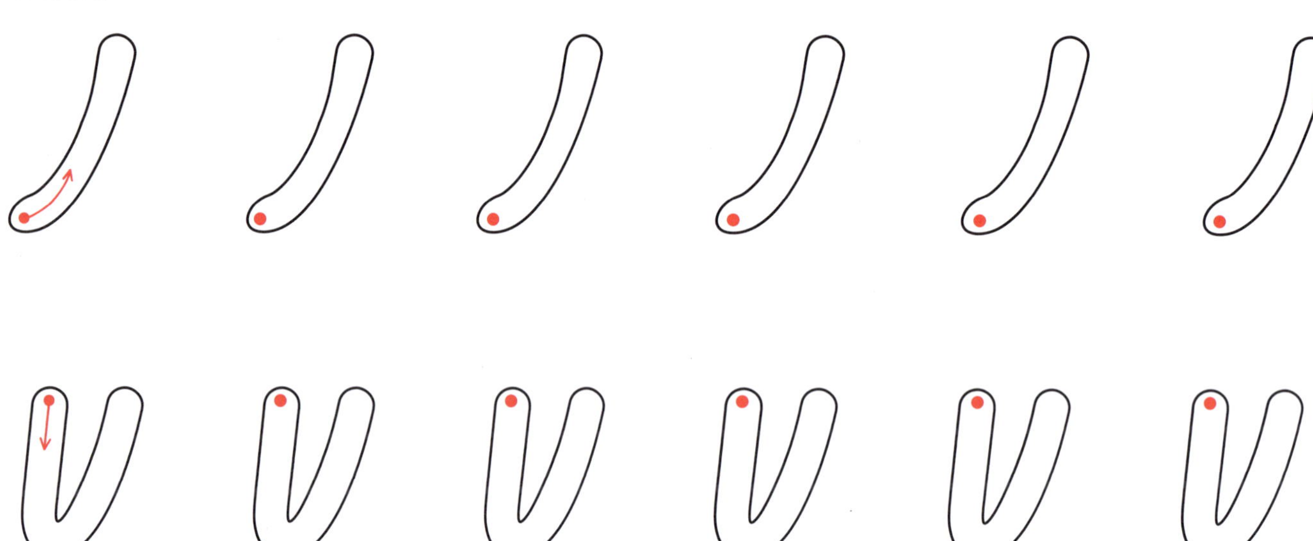

Find 'v'.

Trace and copy. Complete the lines.

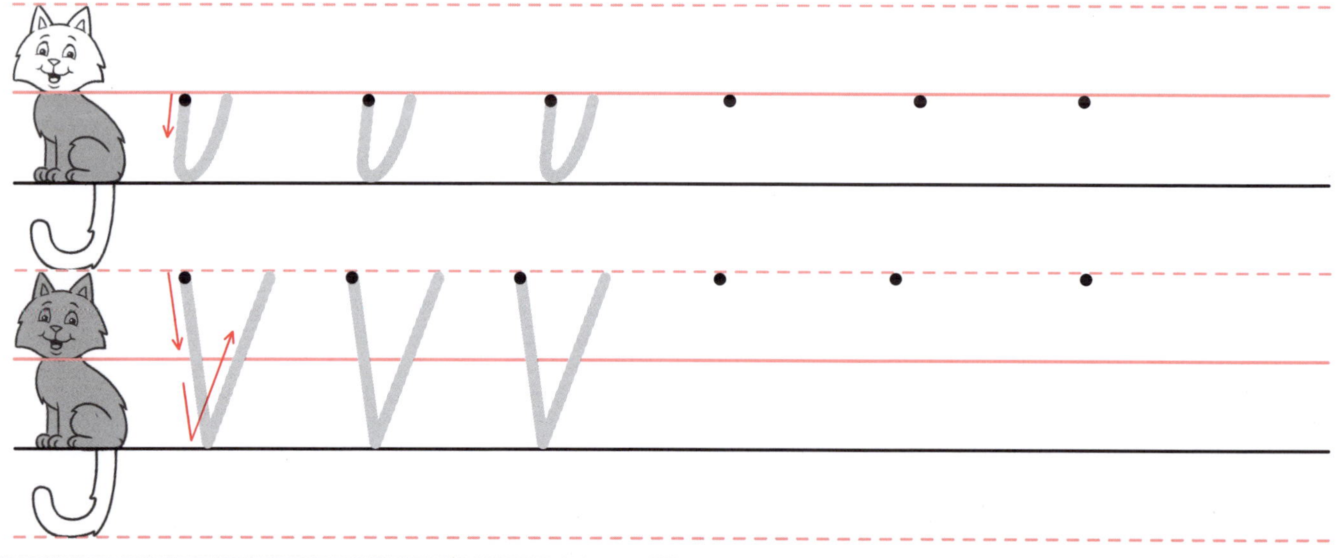

Trace and copy.

very very very

The rain made

the bus very wet.

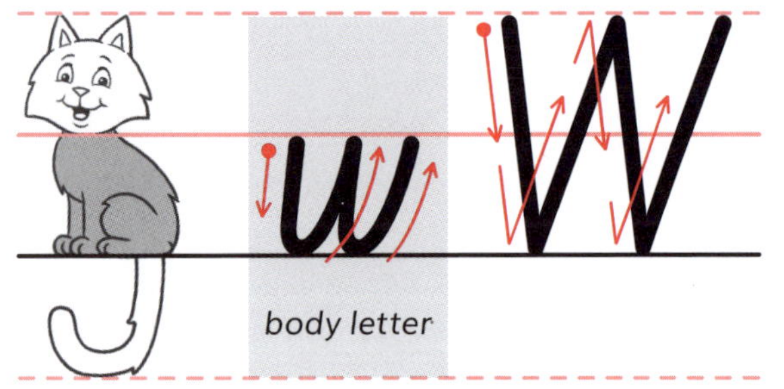

web

Track.

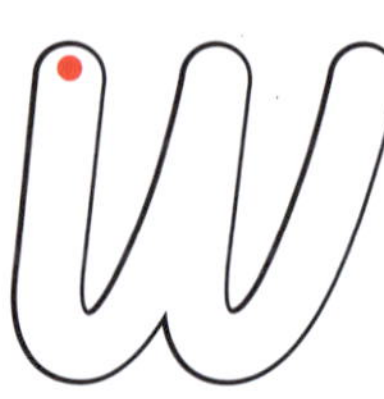

Find 'w' and colour the wedge.

Trace and copy. Complete the lines.

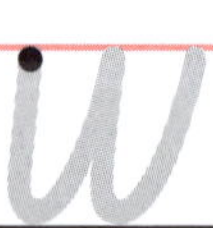

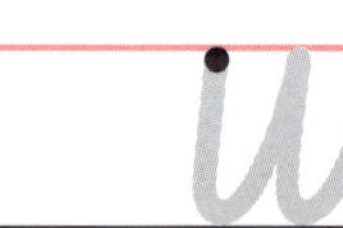

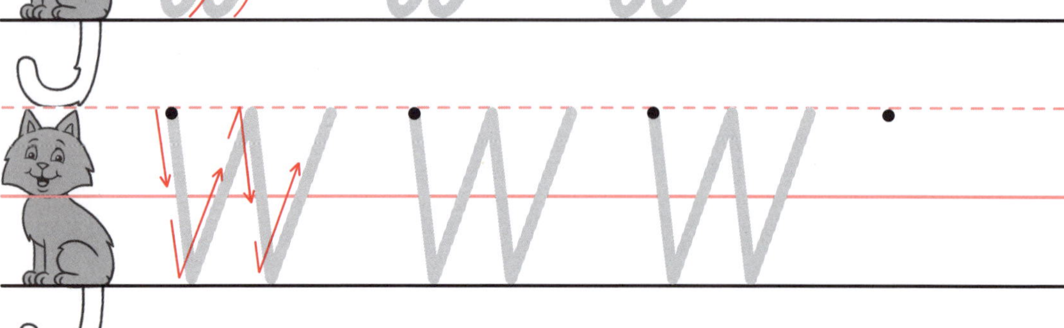

Trace and copy.

will will will will

"I will stop here

for a little rest."

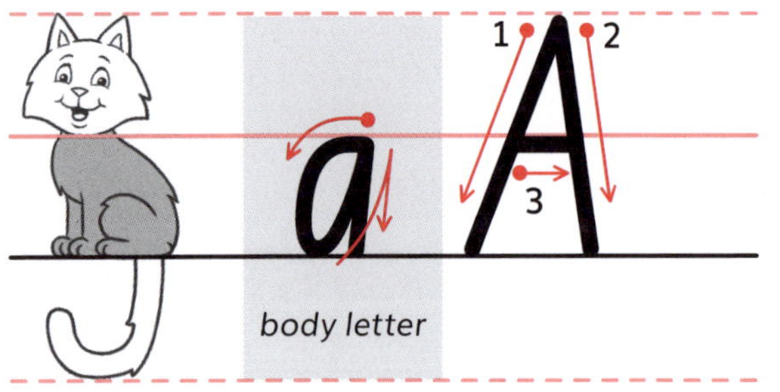

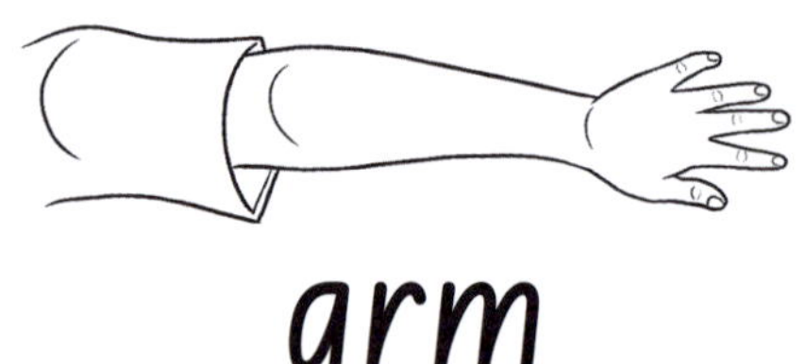

arm

Track.

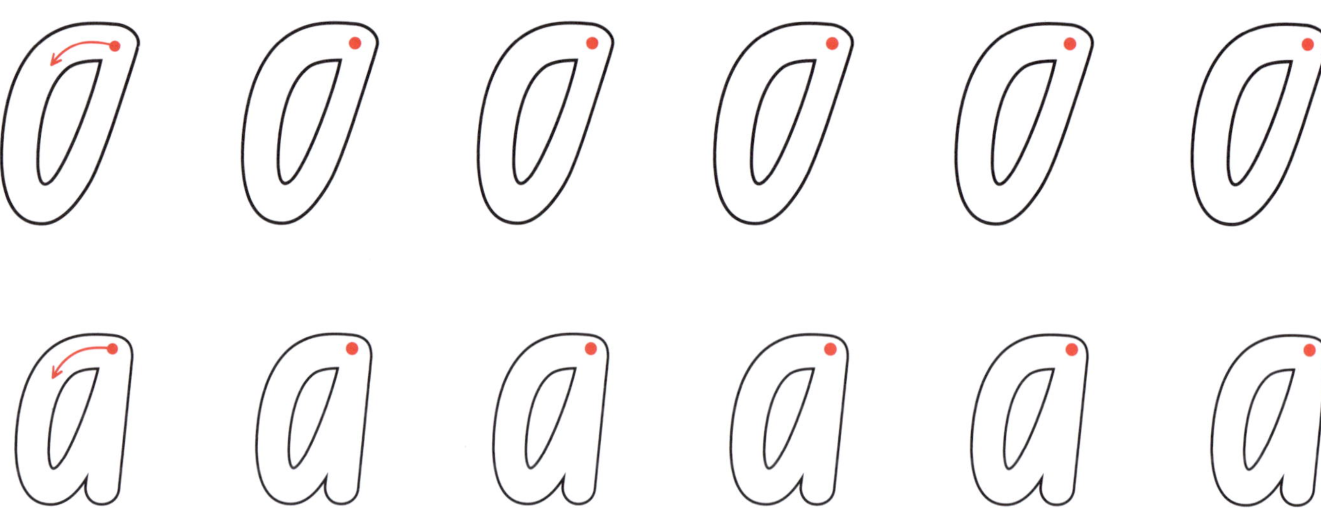

Find 'a' and colour the wedge.

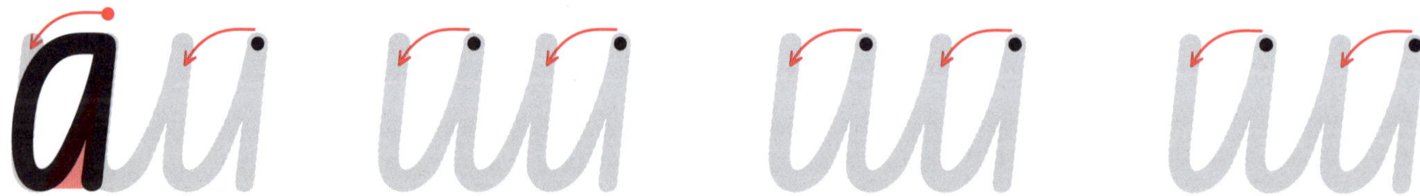

Trace and copy. Complete the lines.

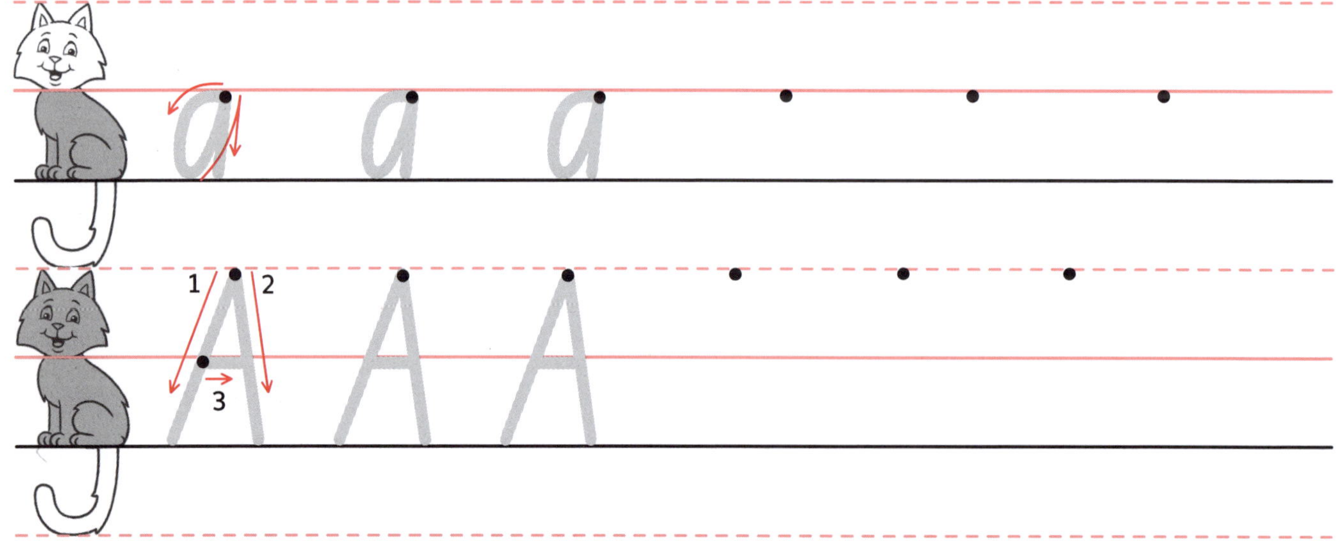

Trace and copy.

asleep asleep asleep

Soon, the Toytown

bus was fast asleep.

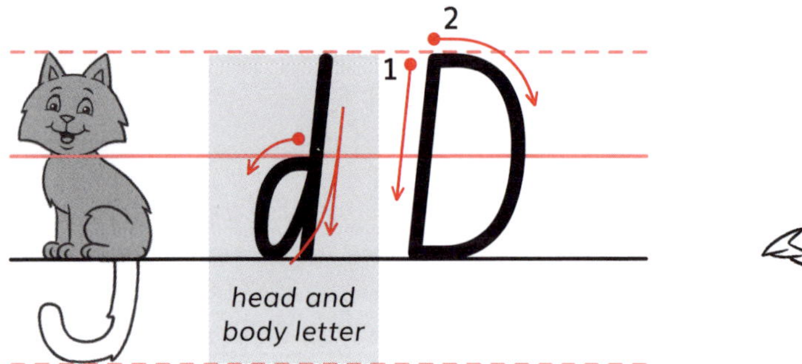

Track.

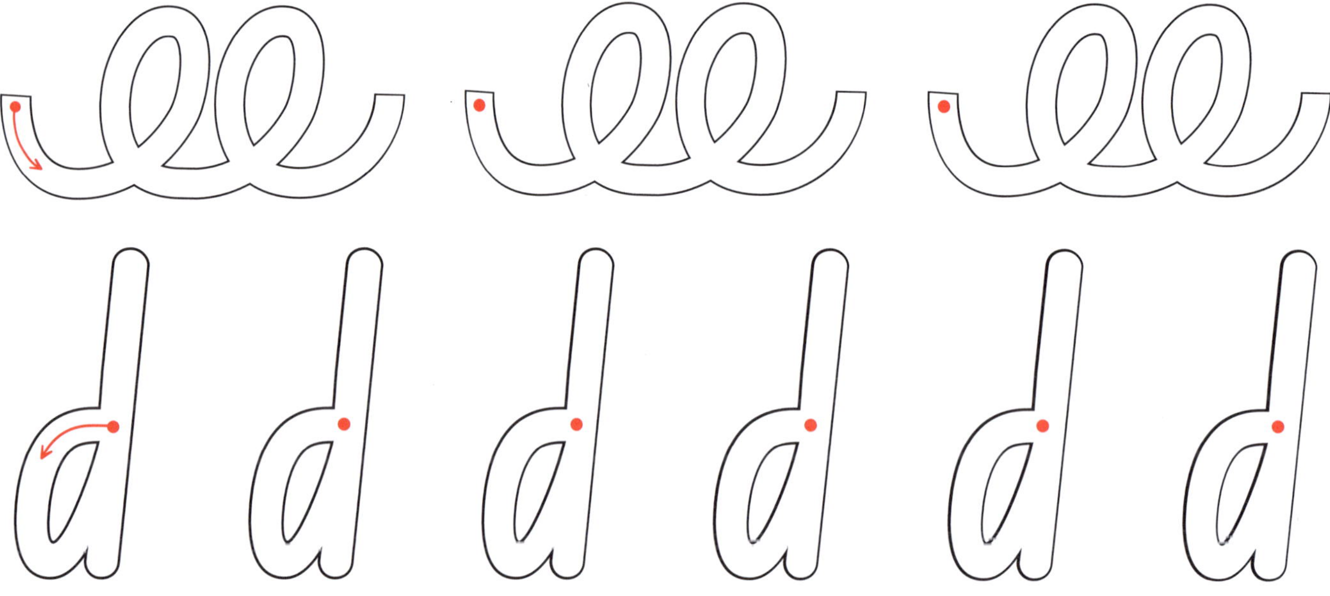

Find 'd' and colour the wedge.

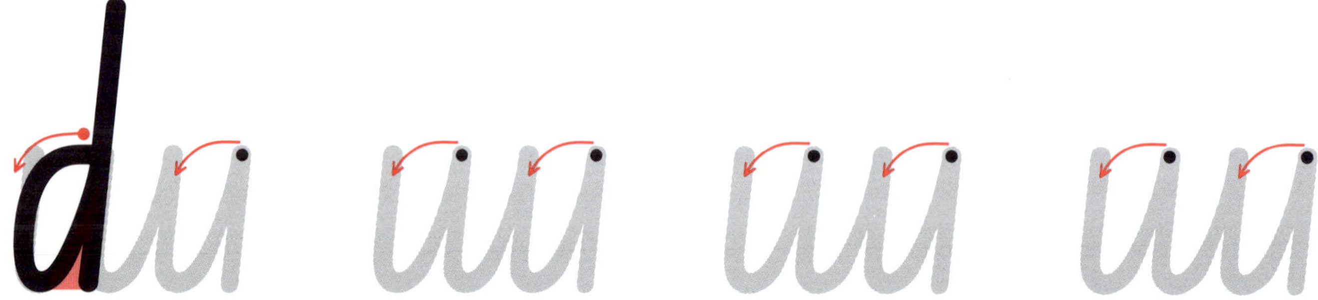

Trace and copy. Complete the lines.

Trace and copy.

down down down

Toytown racing car

came down the hill.

get.ga/PMWA60

Track.

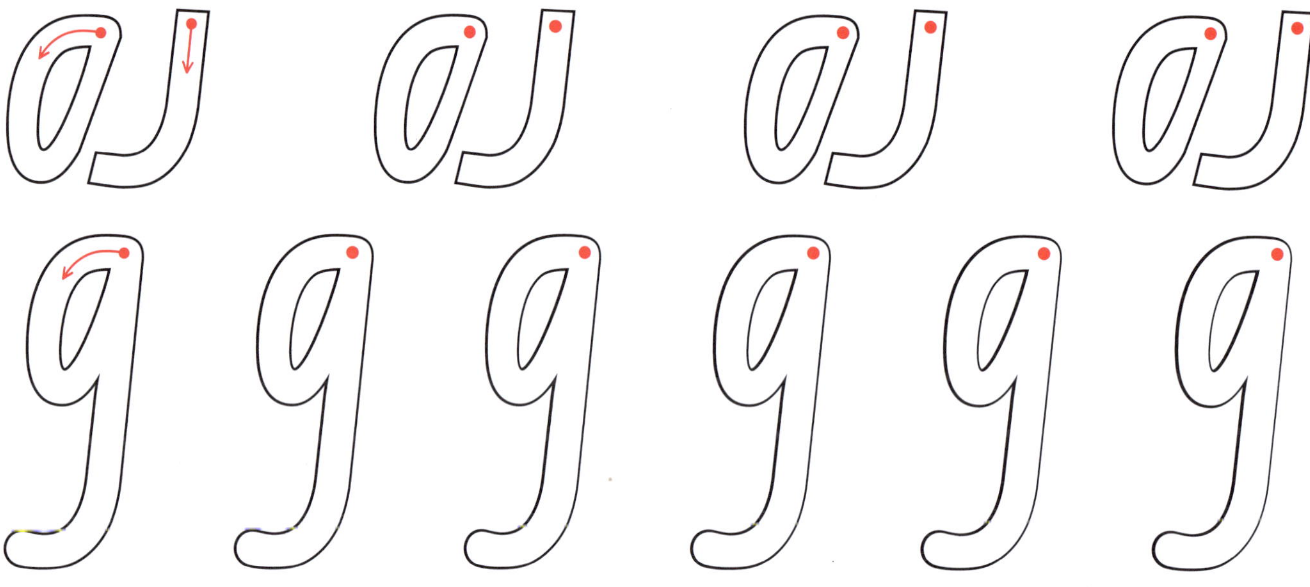

Find 'g' and colour the wedge.

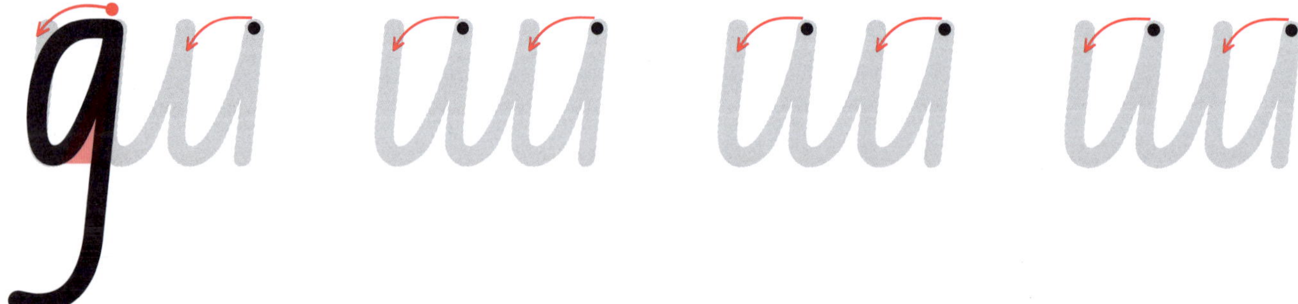

Trace and copy. Complete the lines.

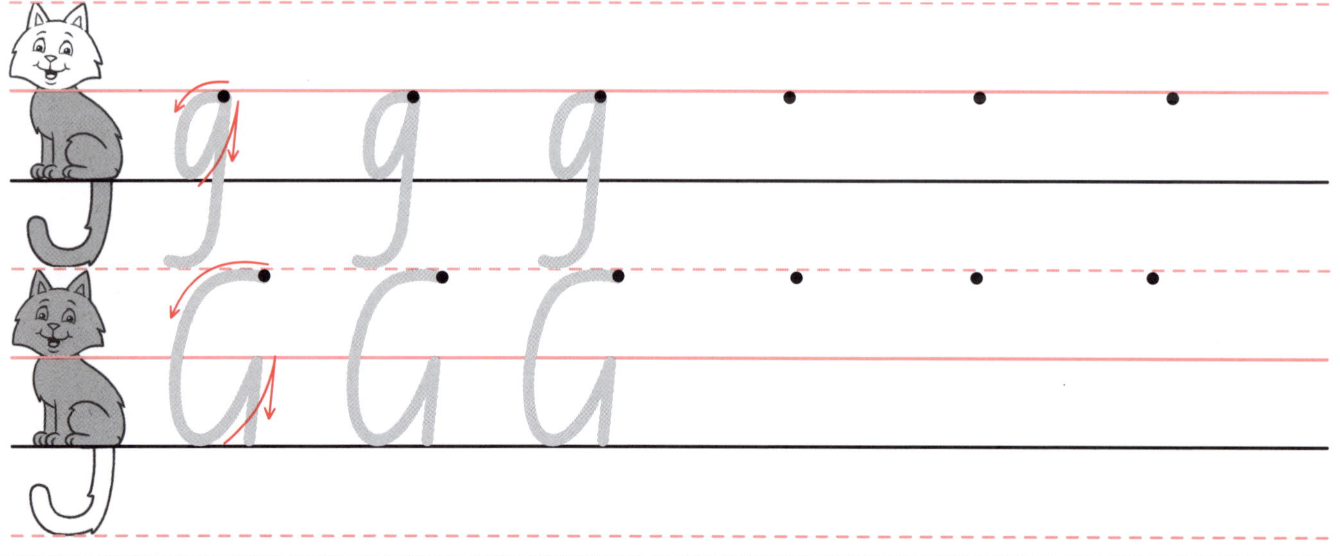

Trace and copy.

Track.

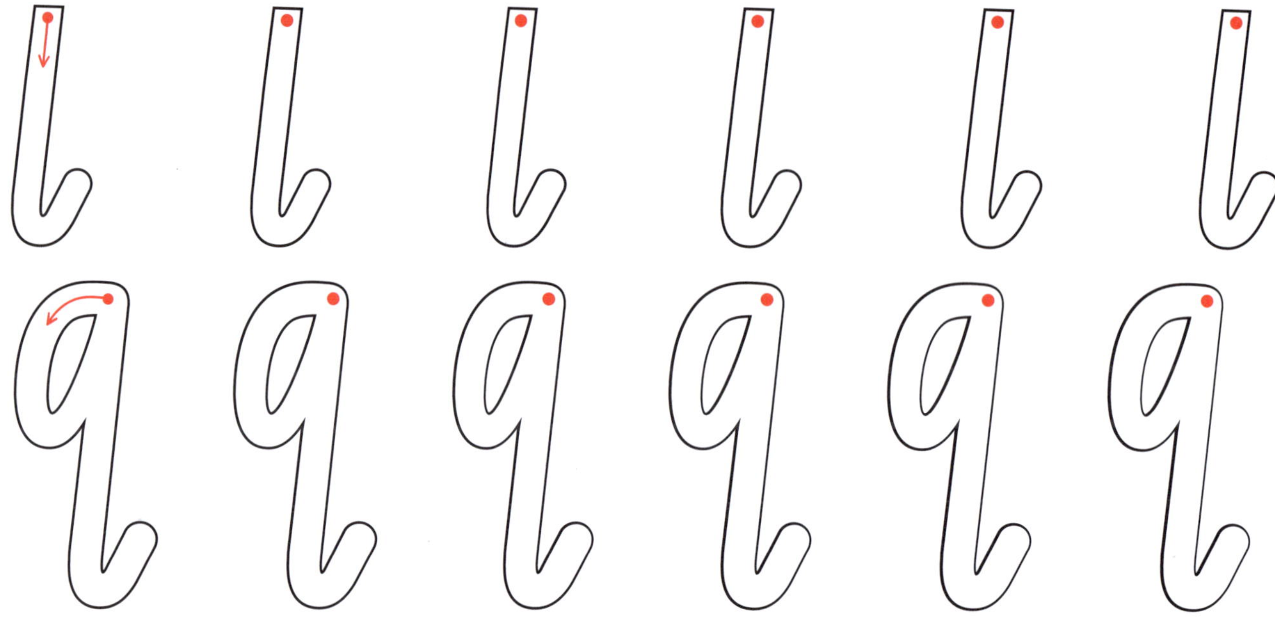

Find '**q**' and colour the wedge.

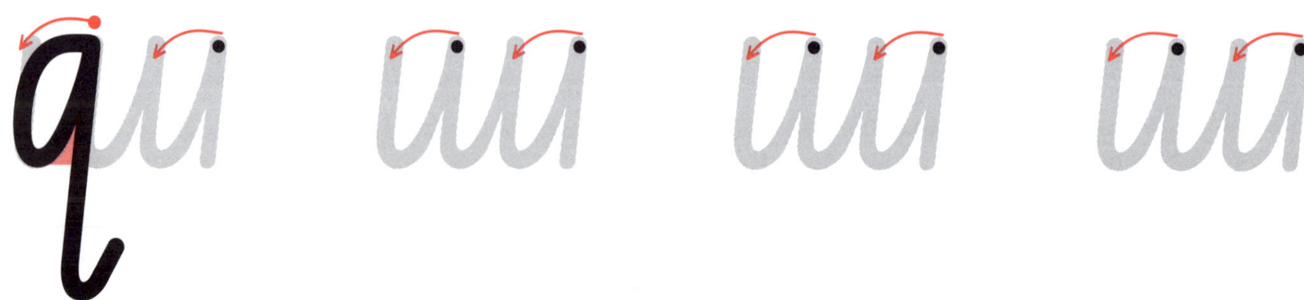

Trace and copy. Complete the lines.

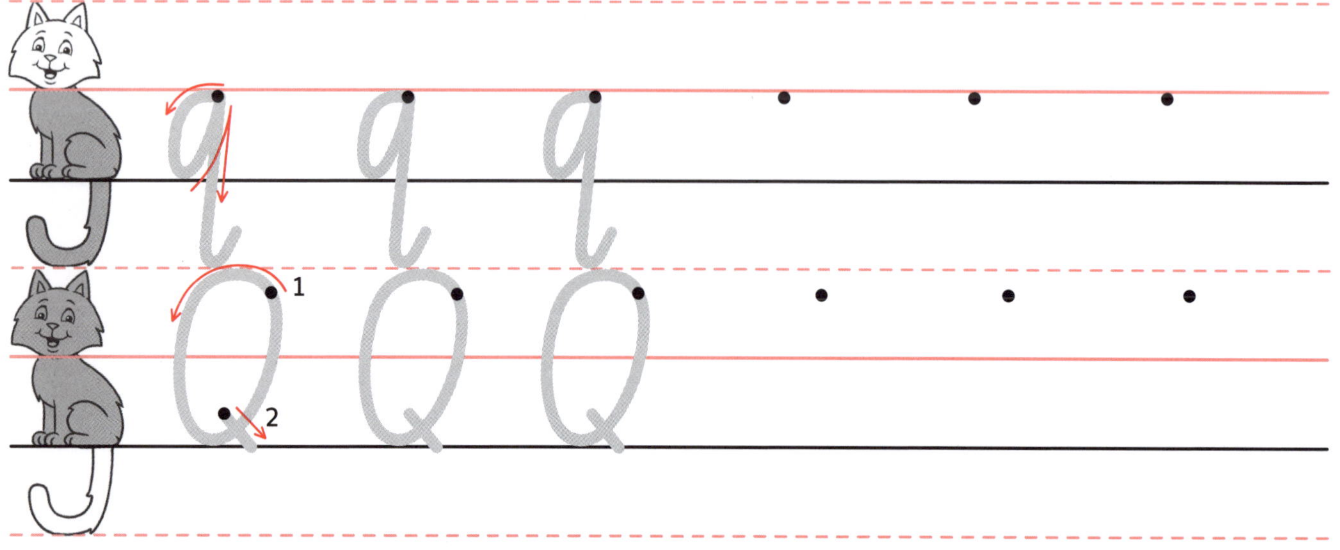

Trace and copy.

get.ga/PMWA61

"Please be quick.

Racing car is stuck!"

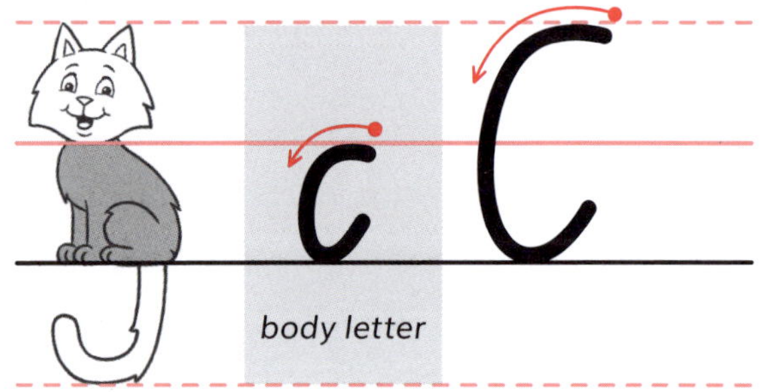

Track.

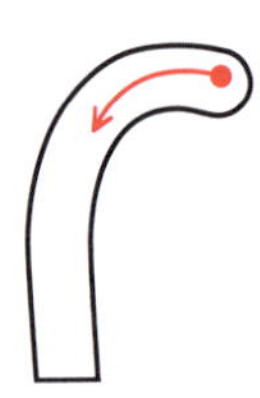

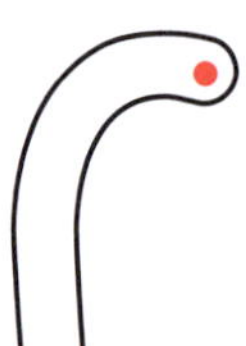

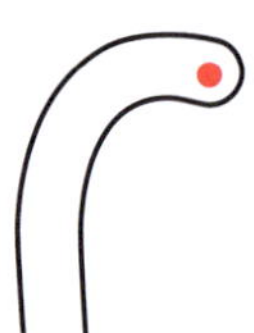

Find 'c'.

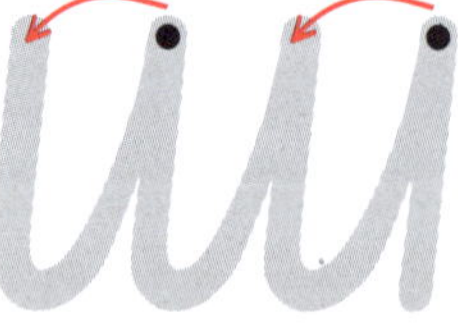

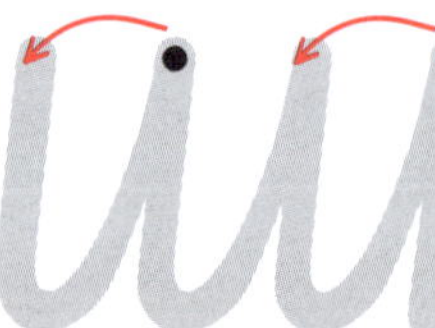

Trace and copy. Complete the lines.

Trace and copy.

came came came

Toytown tow truck

came to the rescue.

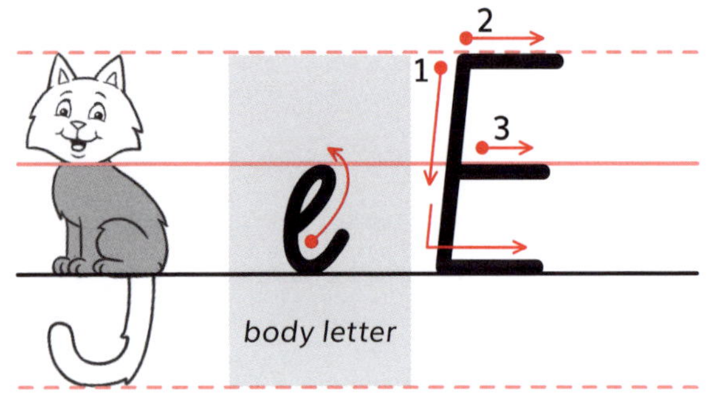

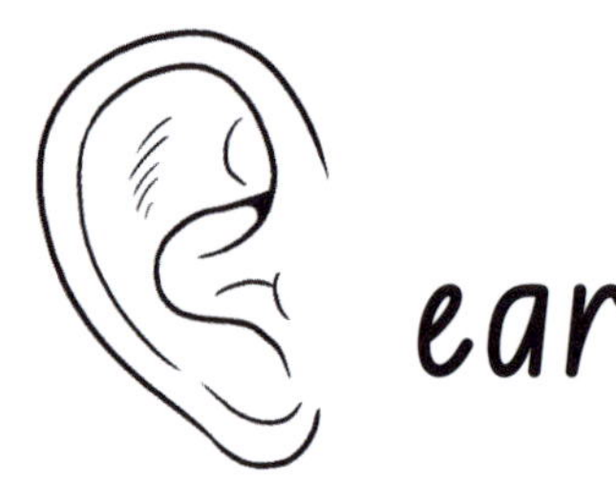

ear

Track.

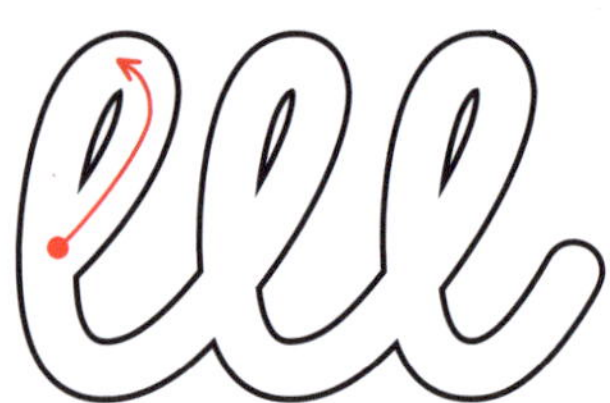

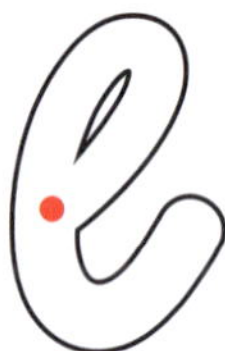

Find 'e'.

Trace and copy. Complete the lines.

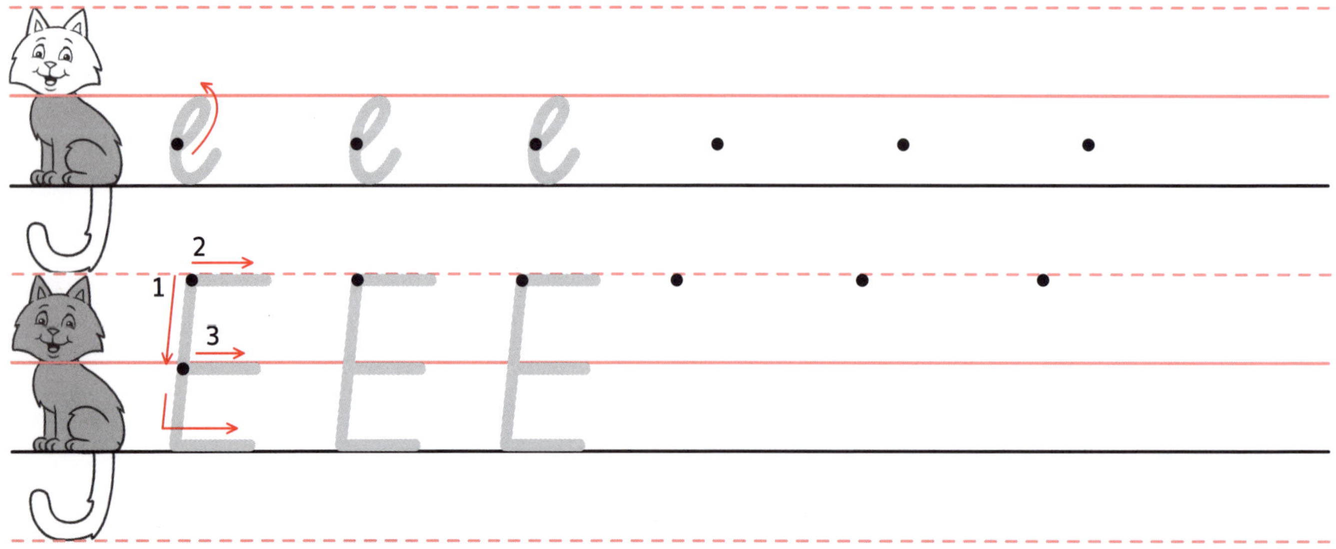

Trace and copy.

end end end end

“Here, take the

end of my rope.”

ISBN: 9780170416894

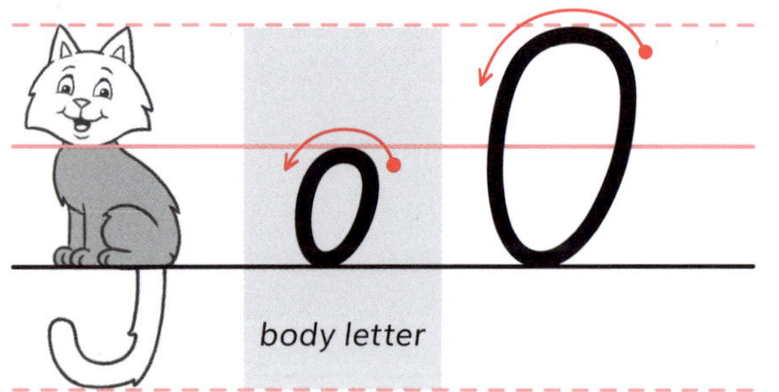

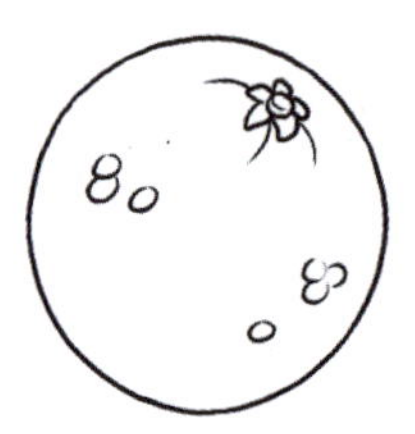

orange

Track.

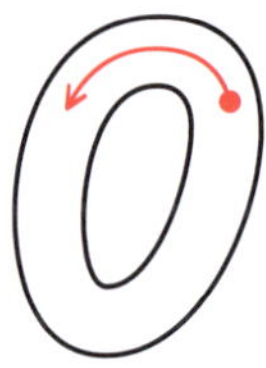

Find 'o'.

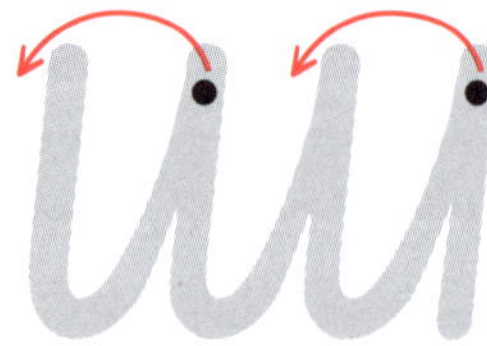

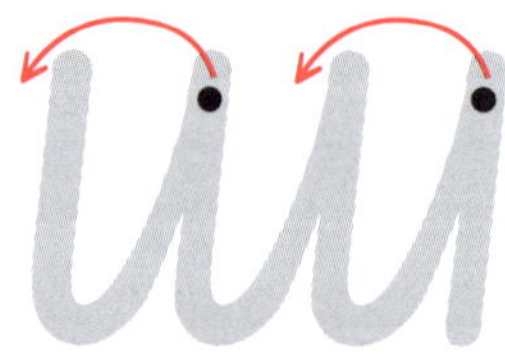

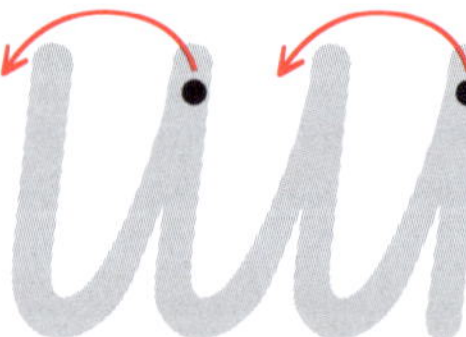

Trace and copy. Complete the lines.

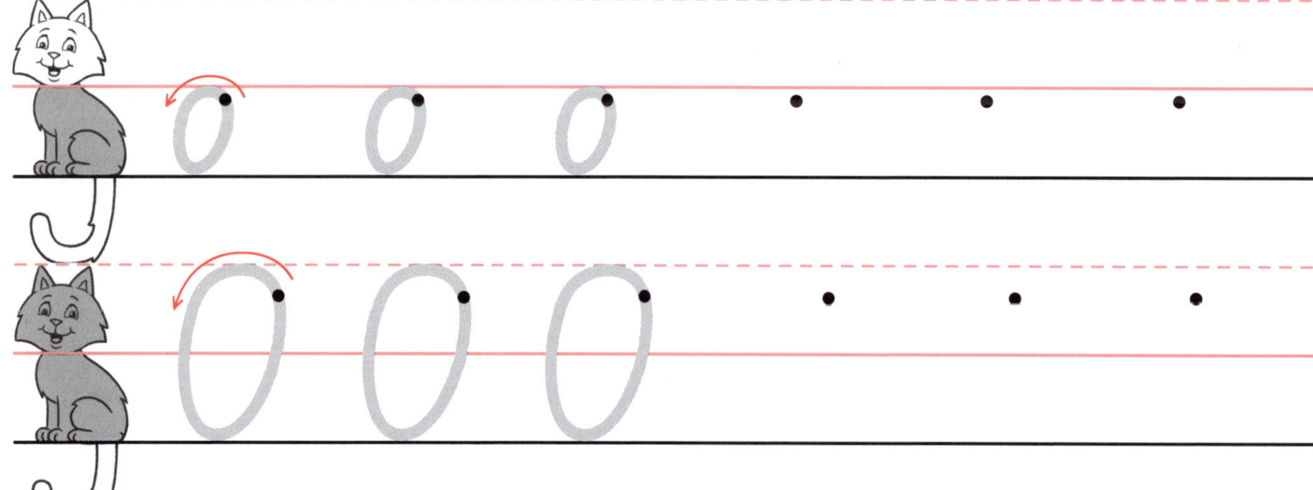

Trace and copy.

out out out out

Tow truck pulled

the racing car out.

ISBN: 9780170416894

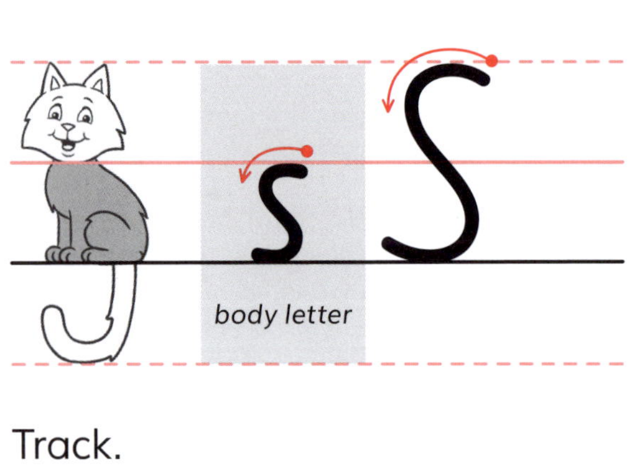

shoe

Track.

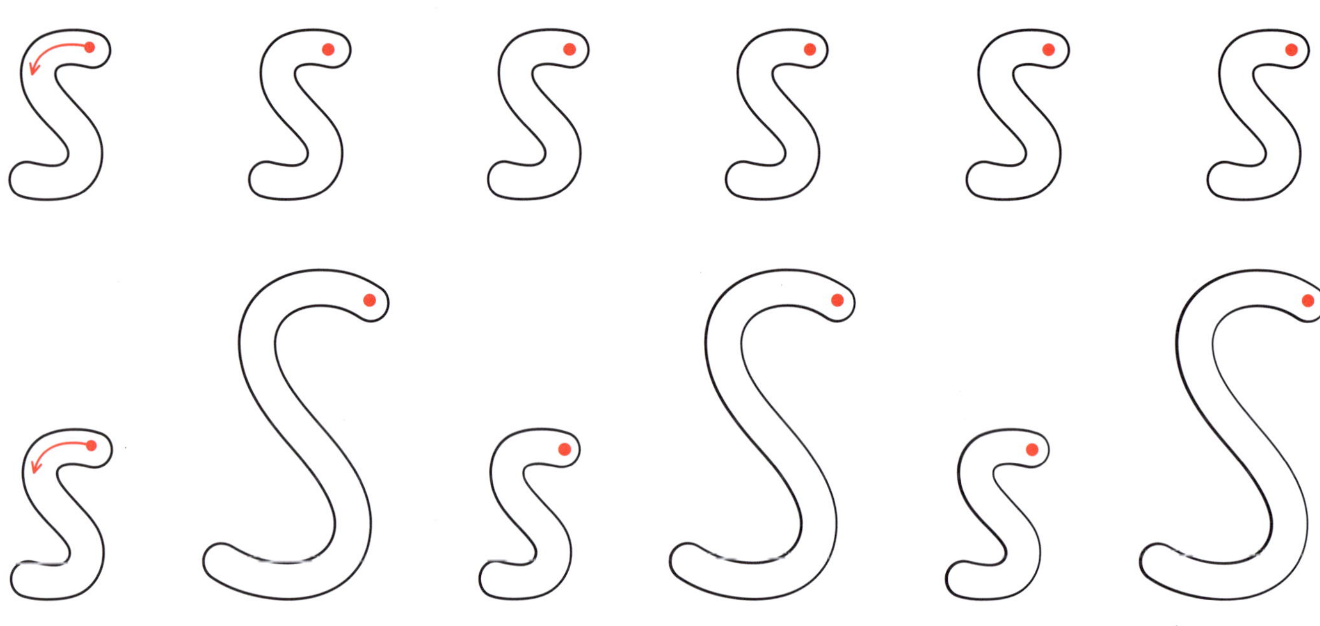

Find 's'.

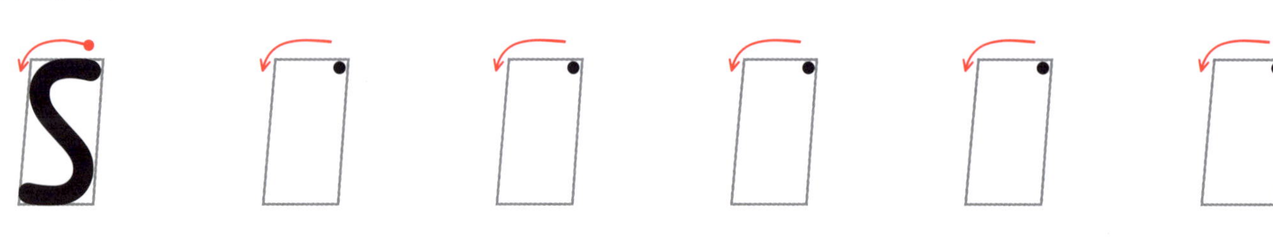

Trace and copy. Complete the lines.

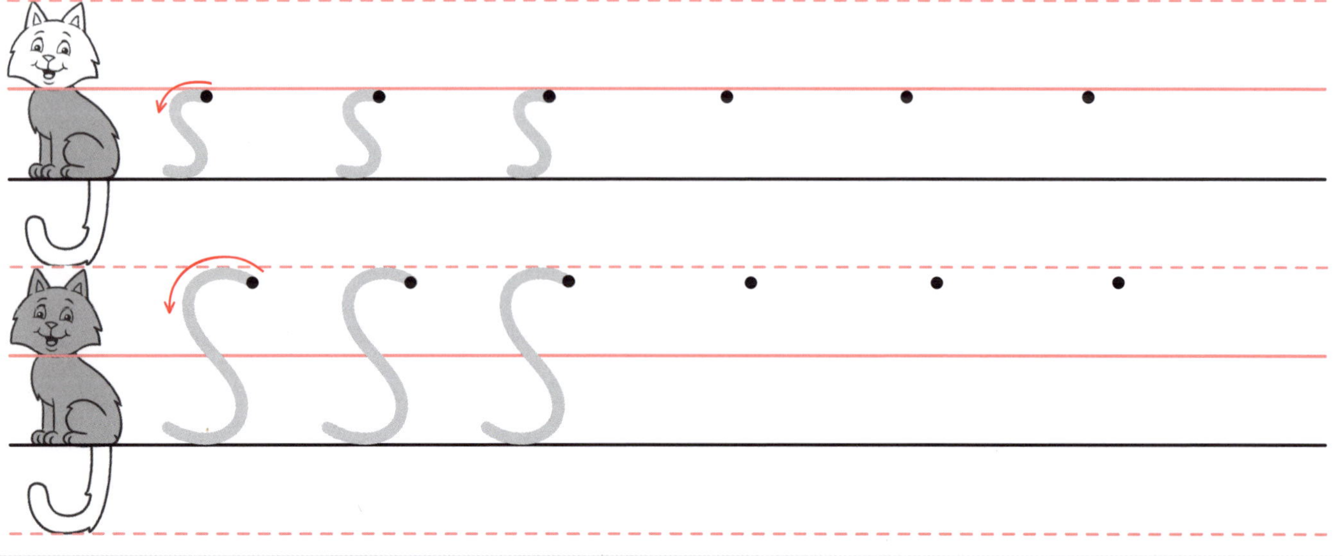

Trace and copy.

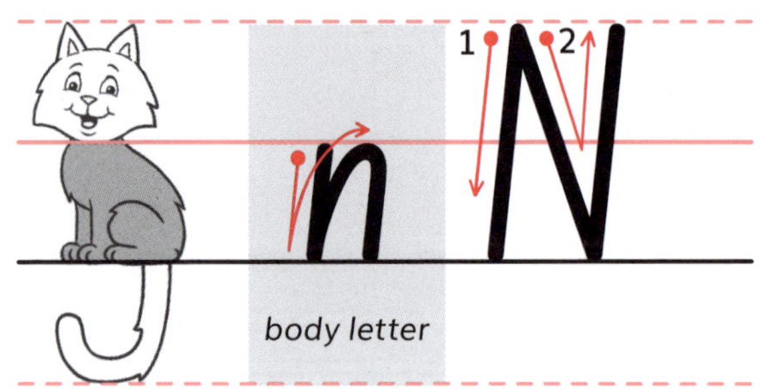

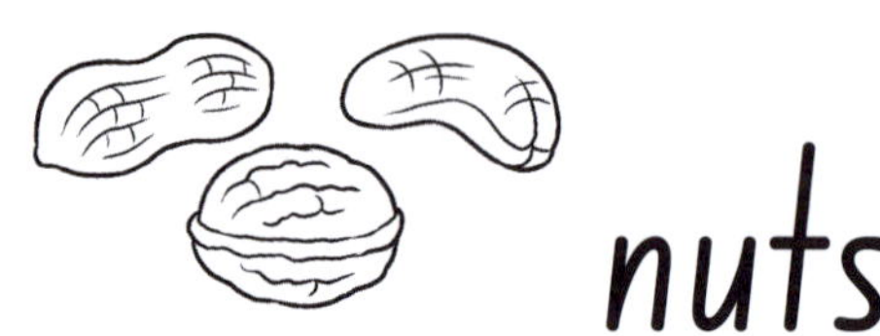

nuts

Track.

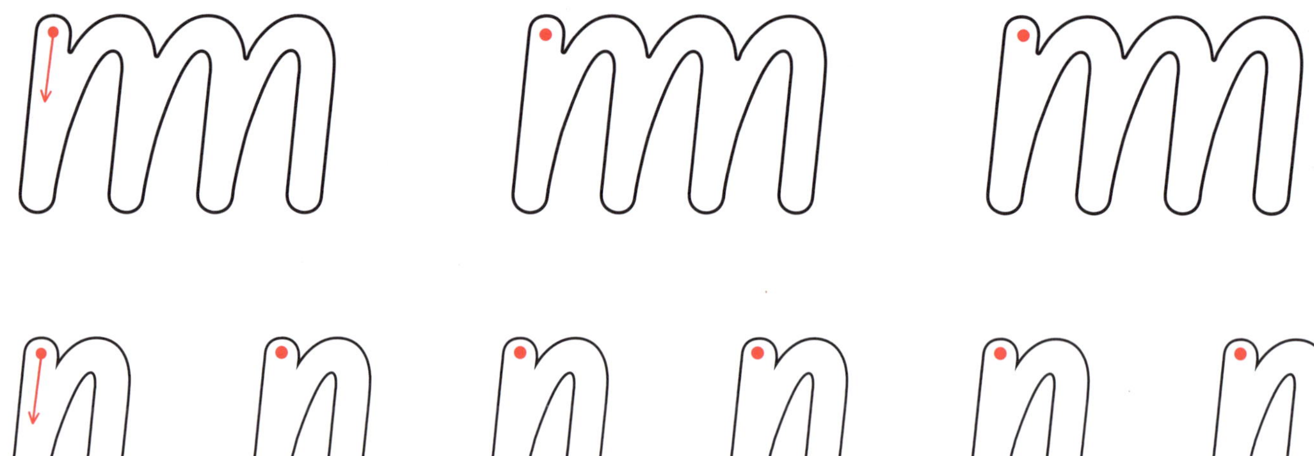

Find 'n' and colour the wedge.

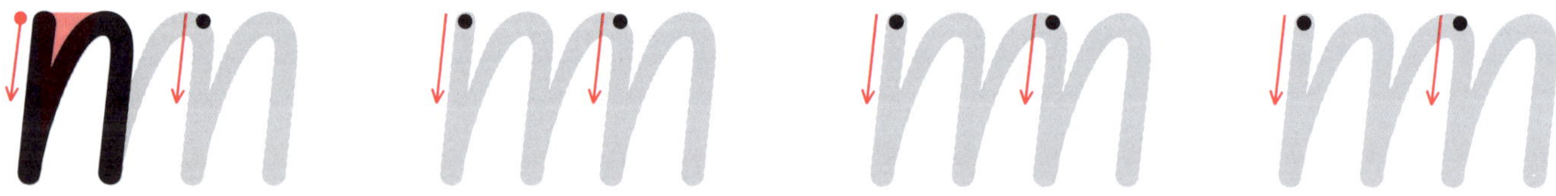

Trace and copy. Complete the lines.

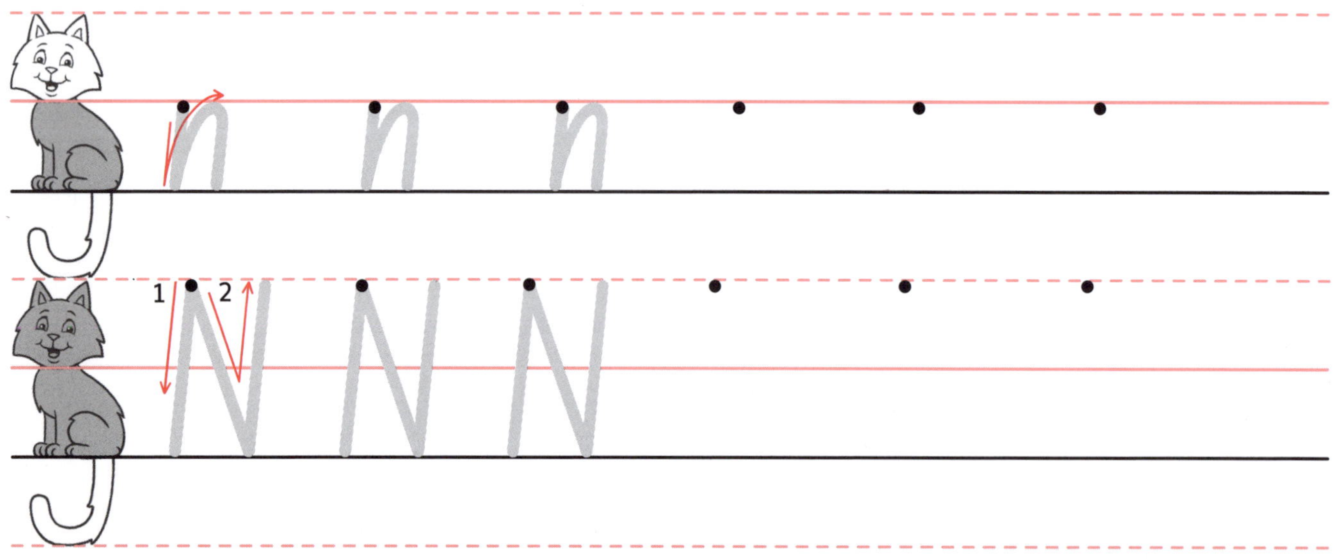

Trace and copy.

near near near

Toytown helicopter

flew near a house.

ISBN: 9780170416894

Track.

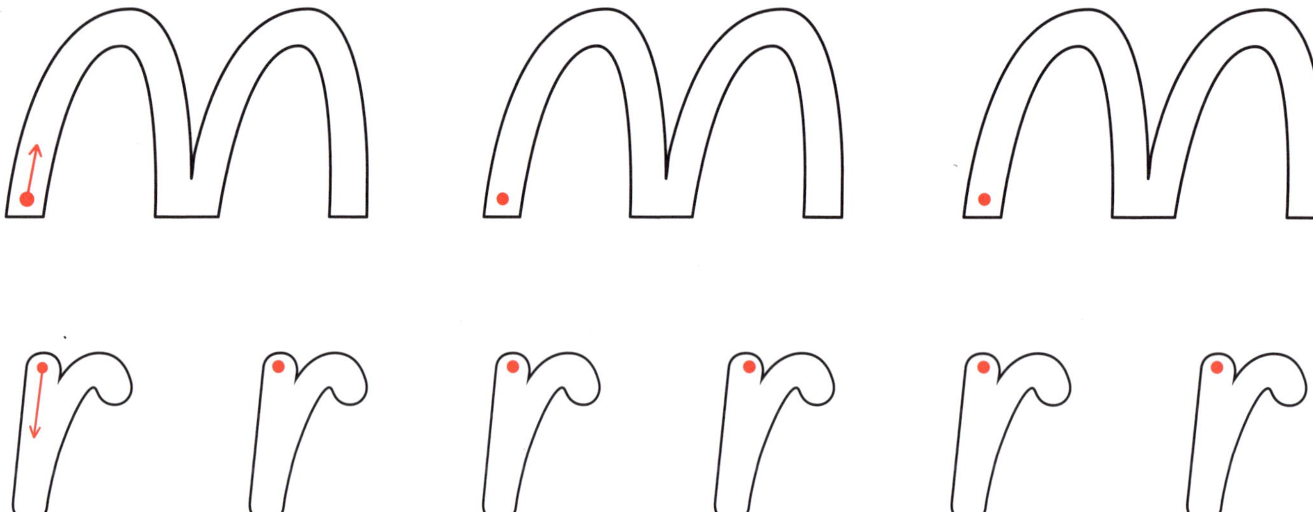

Find ‘r’ and colour the wedge.

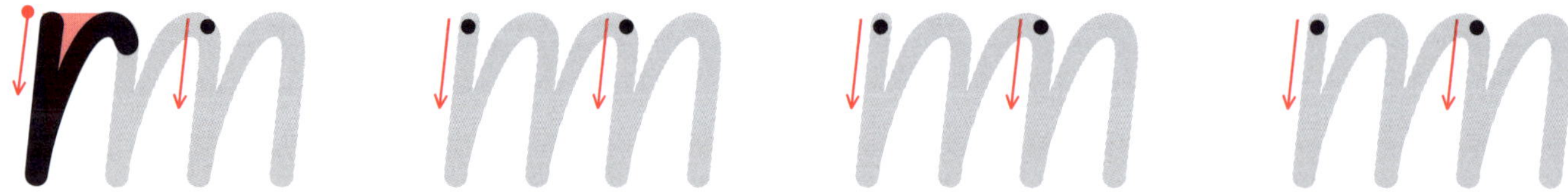

Trace and copy. Complete the lines.

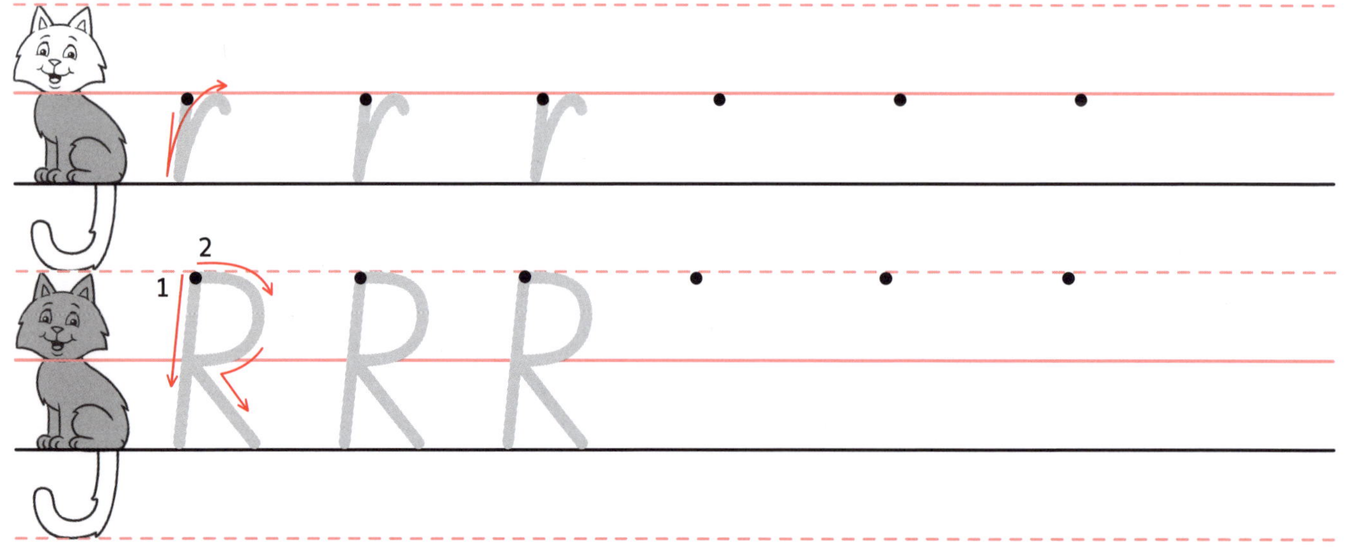

Trace and copy.

roof roof roof

A scared little cat

was on the roof.

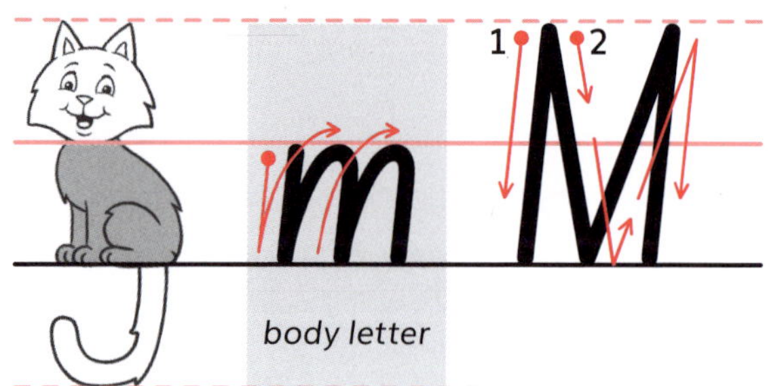

Track.

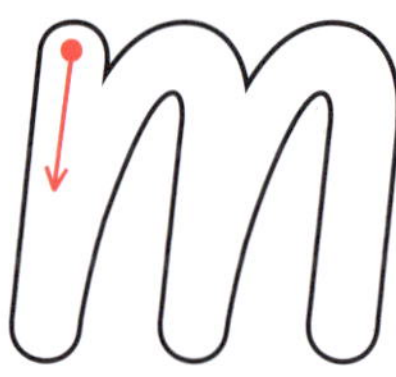 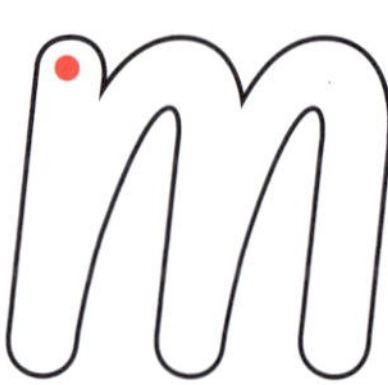  

Find 'm' and colour the wedges.

Trace and copy. Complete the lines.

1 2

Trace and copy.

must must must

"Hurry, fire engine.

You must help."

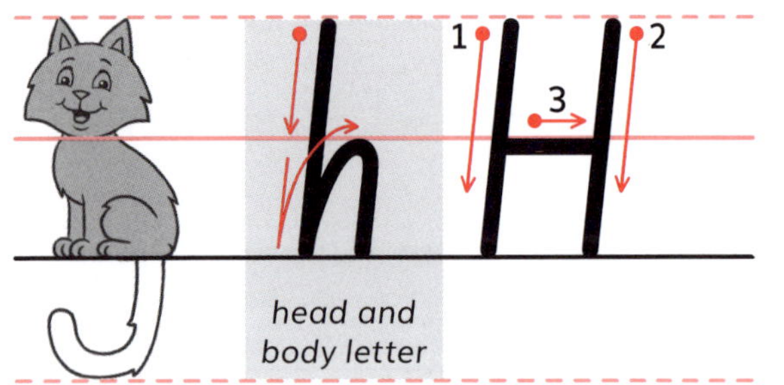

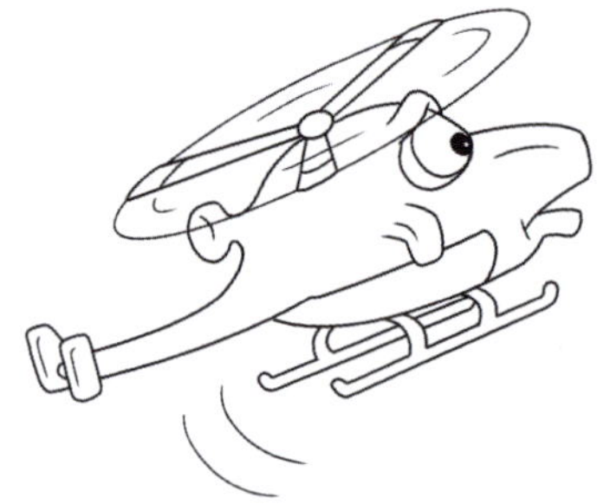

helicopter

Track.

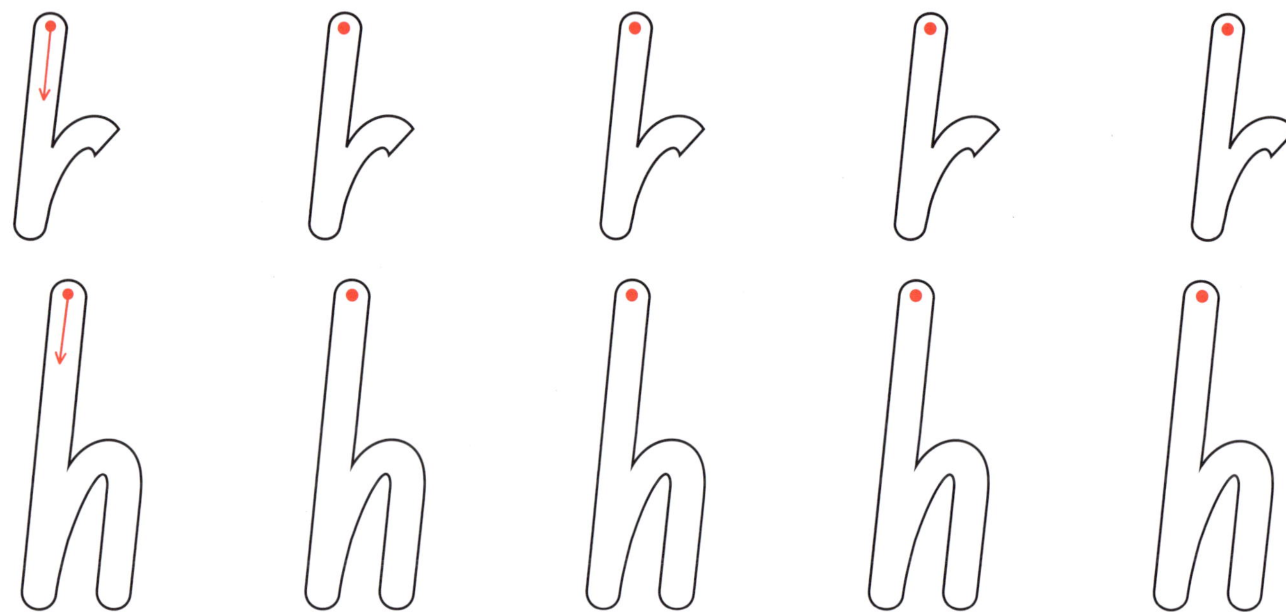

Find 'h' and colour the wedge.

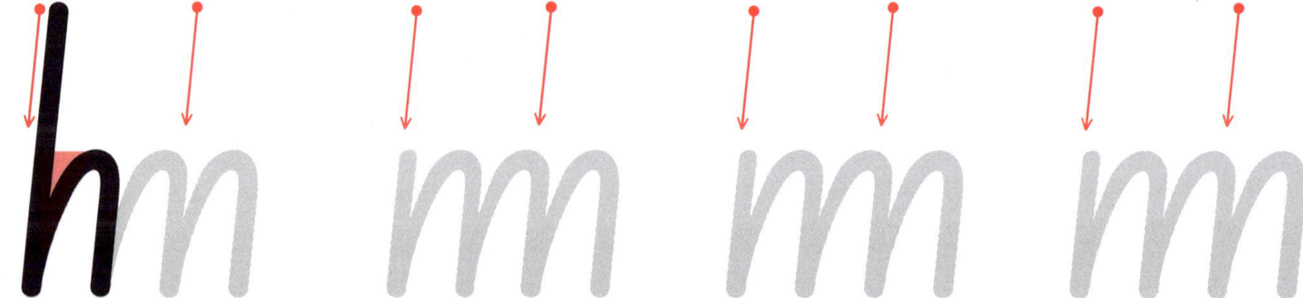

Trace and copy. Complete the lines.

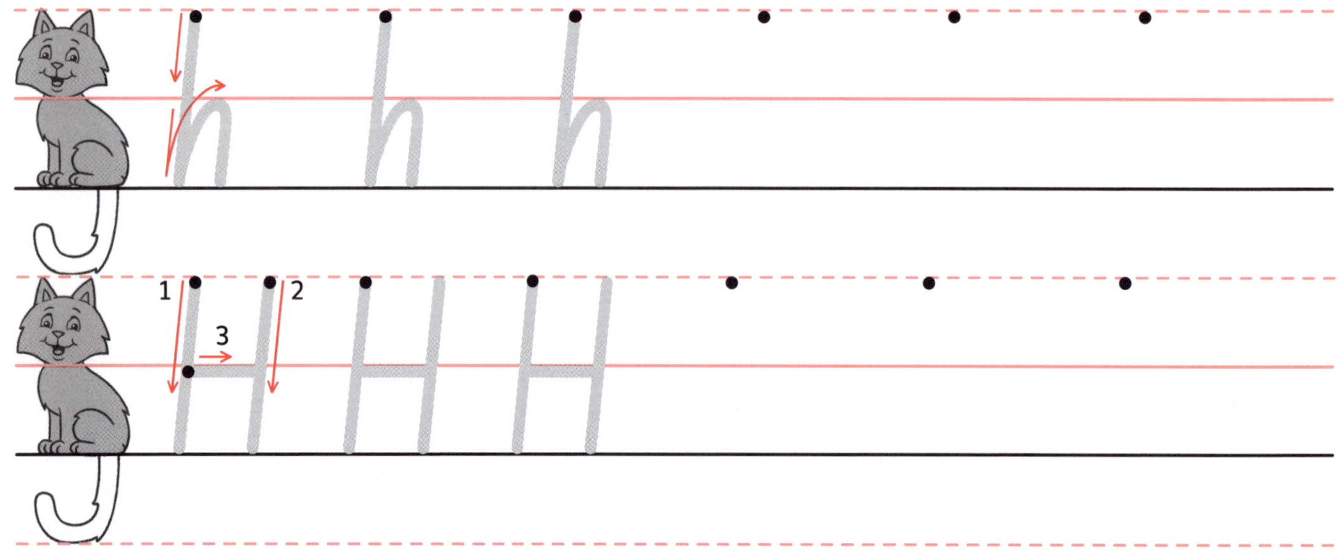

Trace and copy.

here here here

get.ga/PMWA63

“A little cat is here

on the roof.”

ISBN: 9780170416894

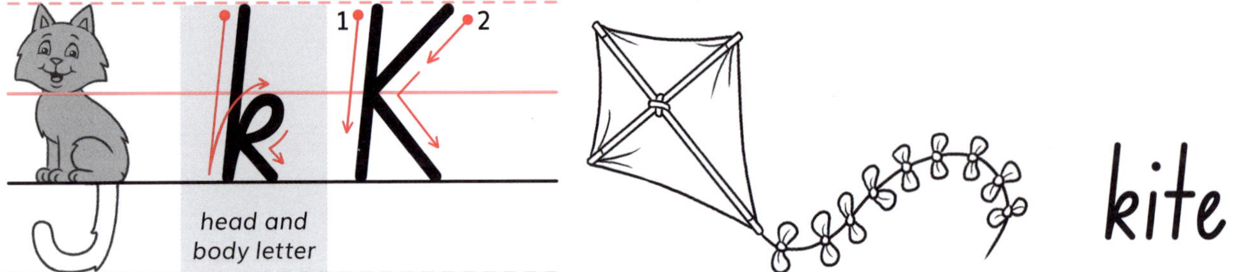

Track.

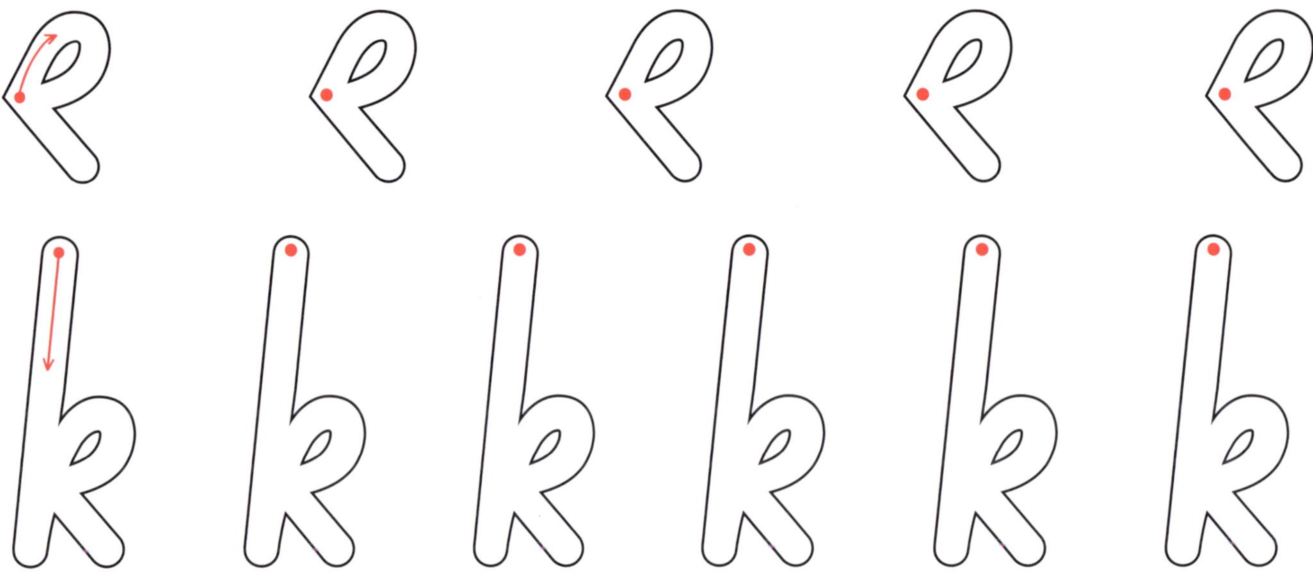

Find ‘k’ and colour the wedge.

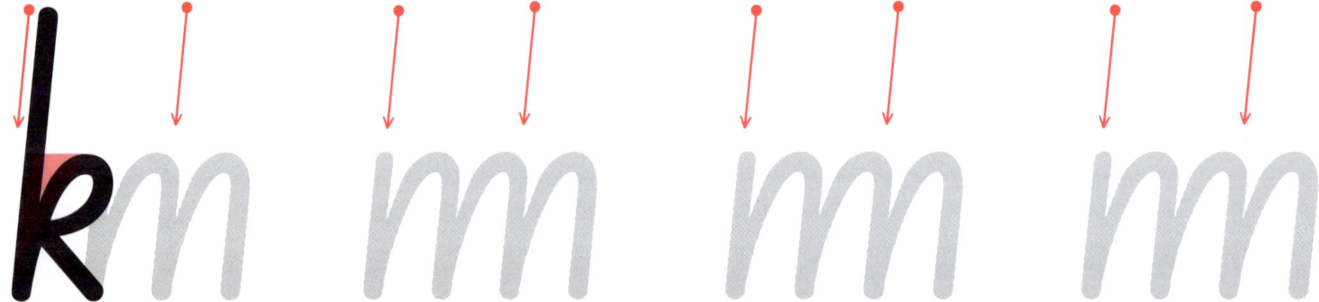

Trace and copy. Complete the lines.

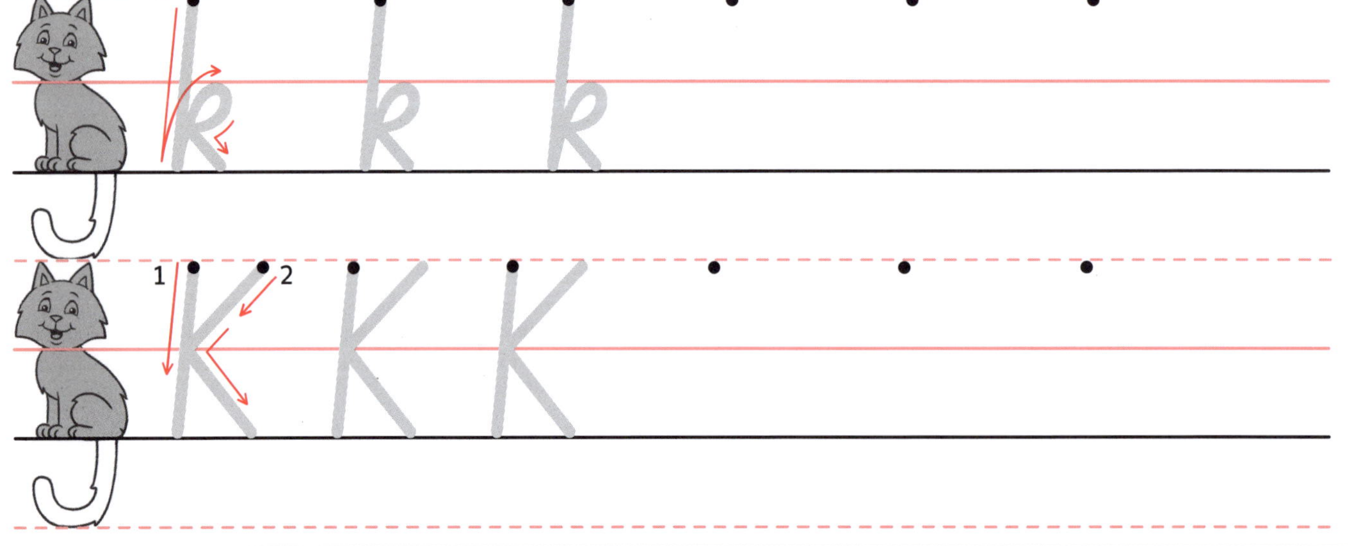

Trace and copy.

keep keep keep

"Little cat, keep still.

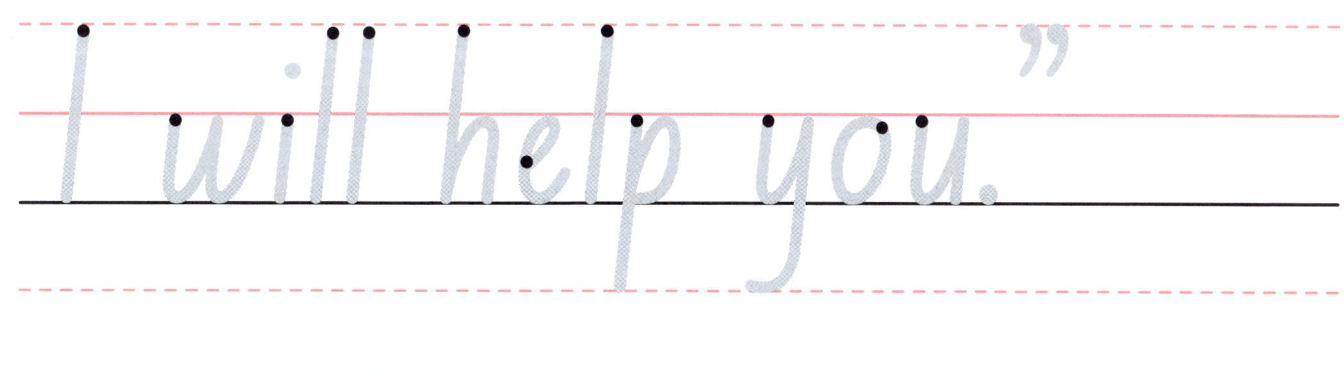

I will help you."

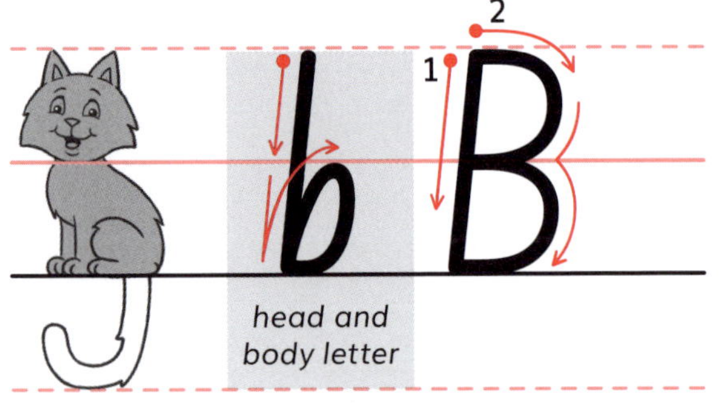

bear

Track.

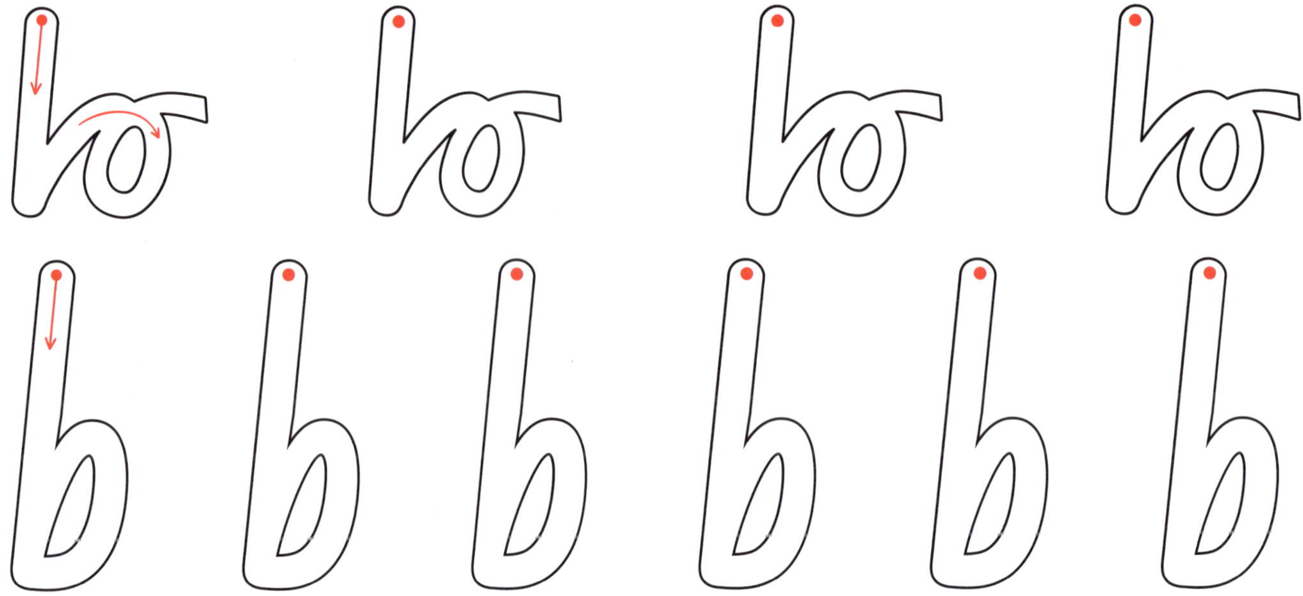

Find 'b' and colour the wedge.

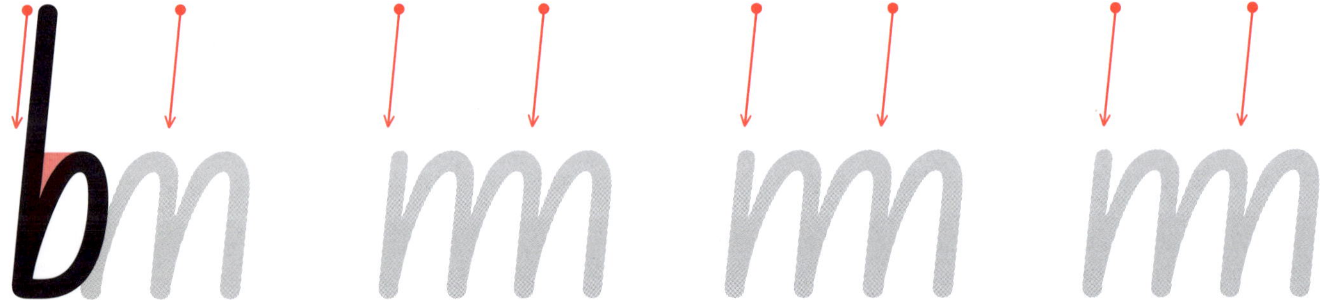

Trace and copy. Complete the lines.

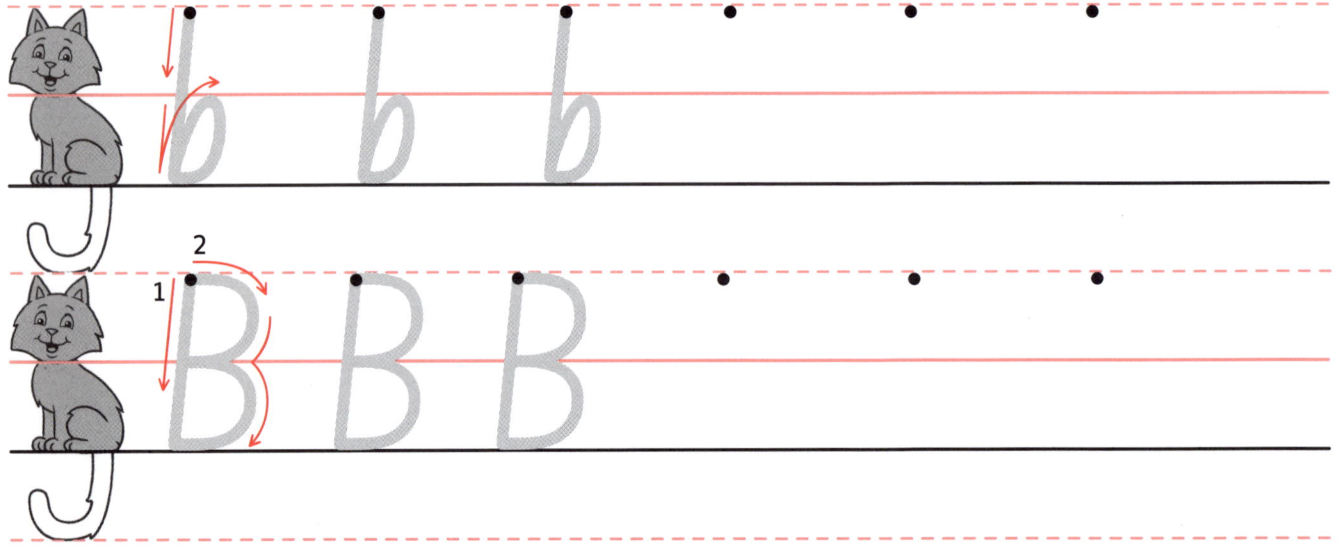

Trace and copy.

Fire engine stopped

beside the house.

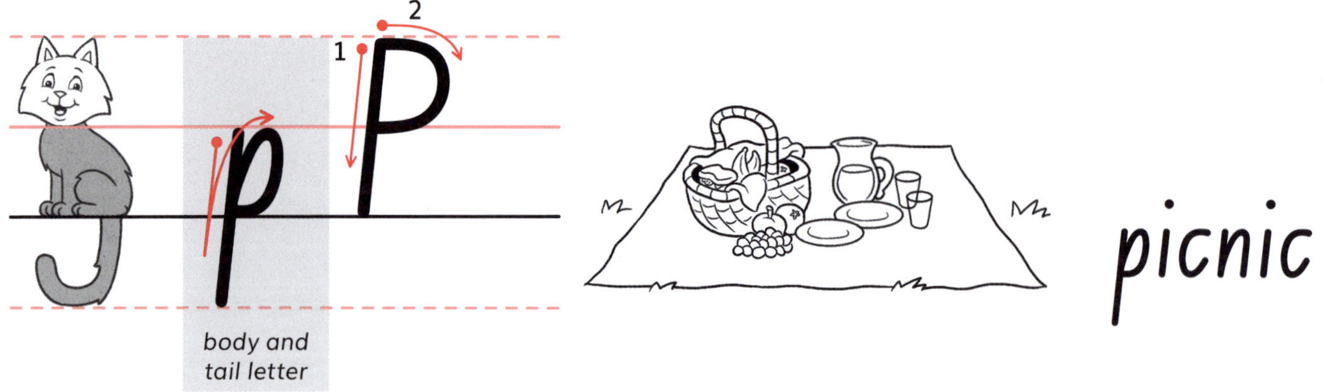

Track.

Find 'p' and colour the wedge.

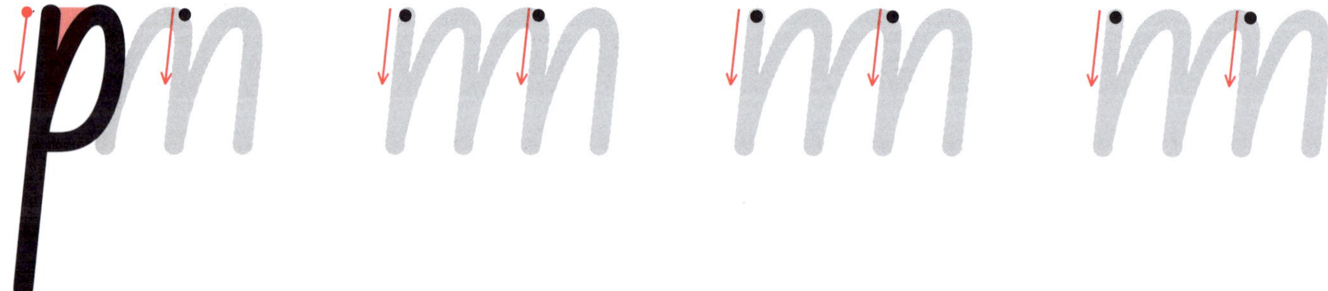

Trace and copy. Complete the lines.

Trace and copy.

put put put put

“I will put her here,”

said the fire engine.

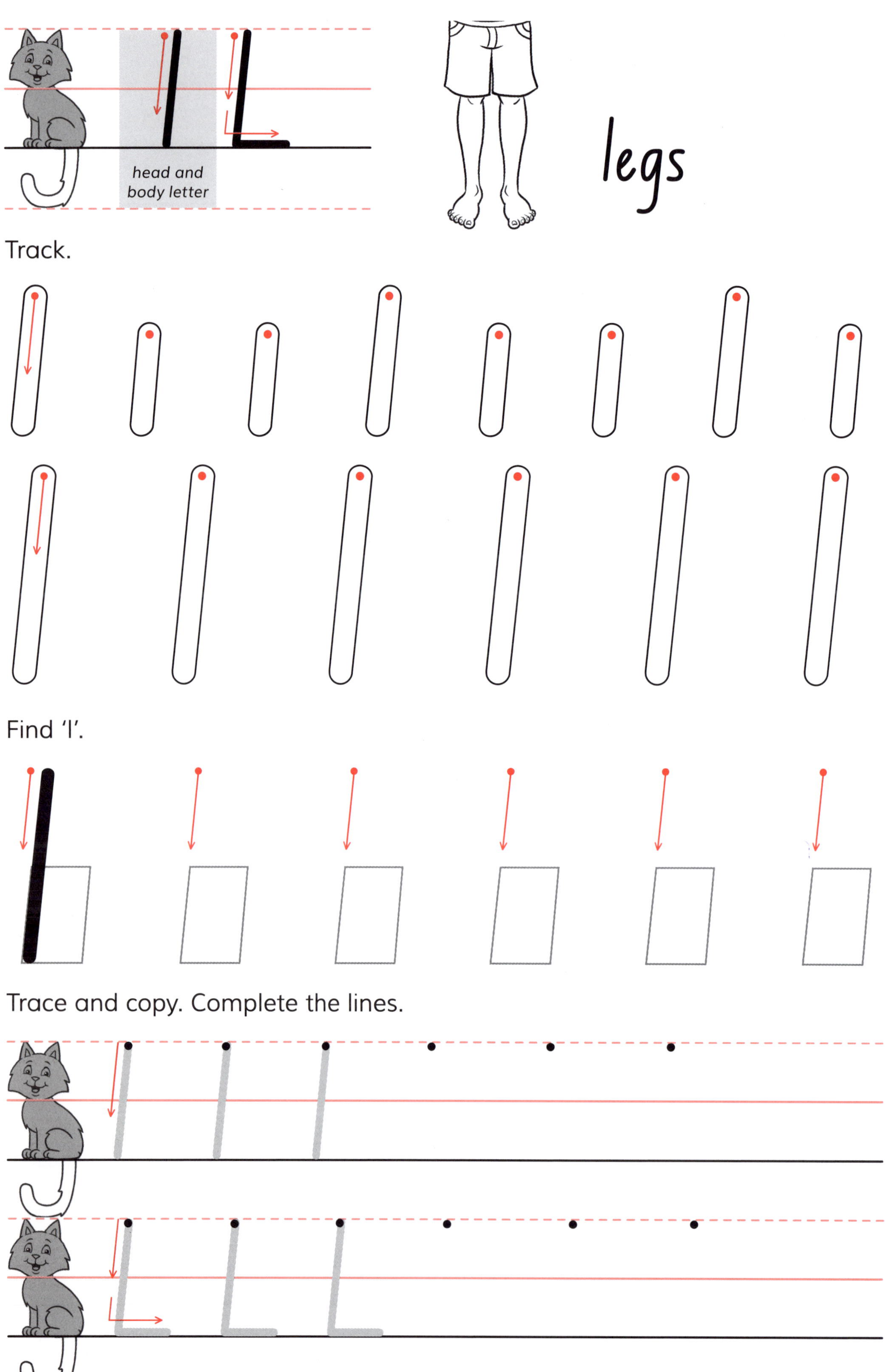

Track.

Find 'l'.

Trace and copy. Complete the lines.

Trace and copy.

looked looked

The bus looked at

the tow truck's tyre.

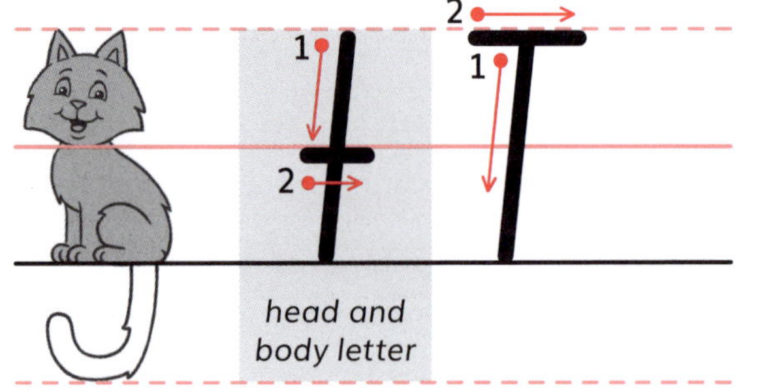

train

Track.

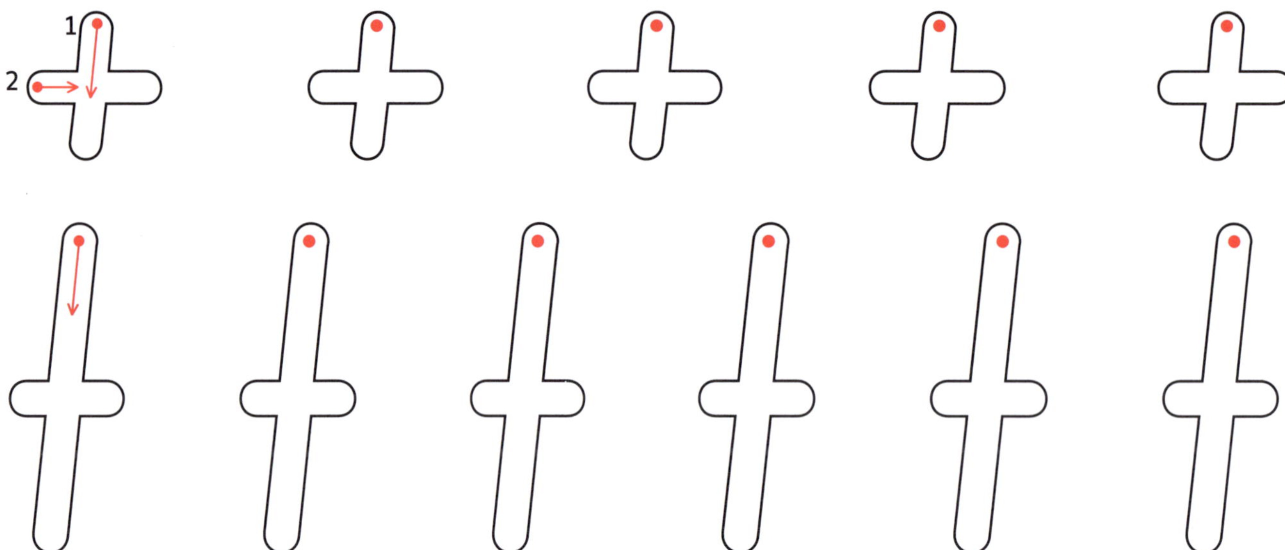

Find 't'.

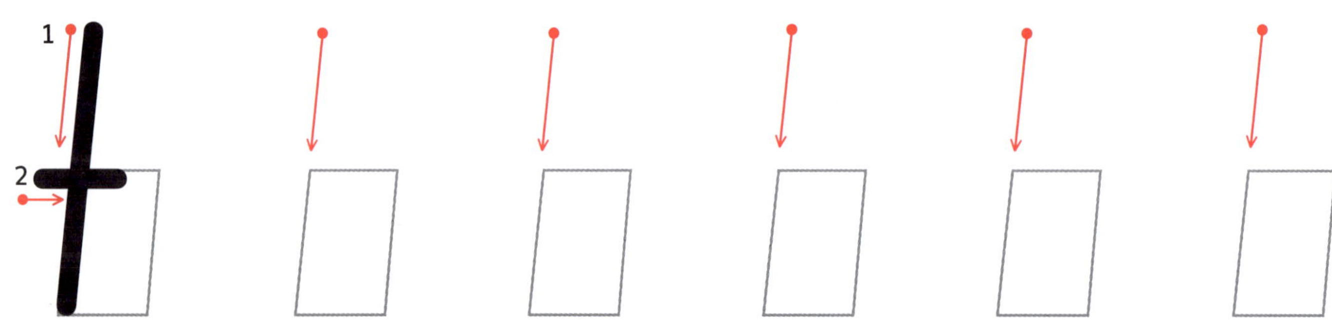

Trace and copy. Complete the lines.

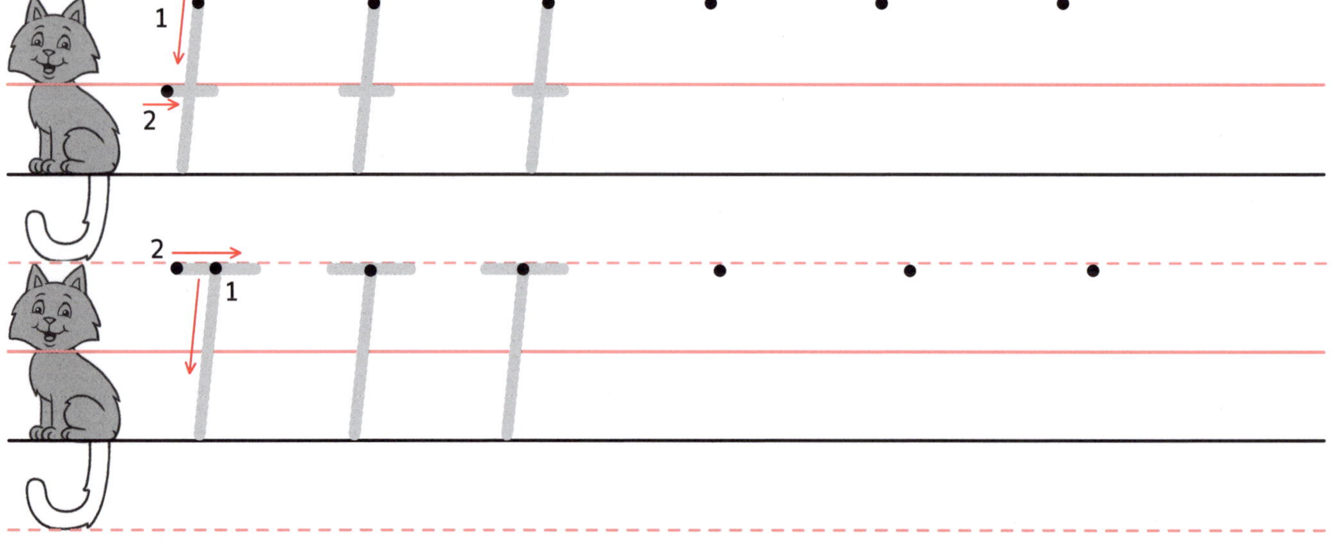

Trace and copy.

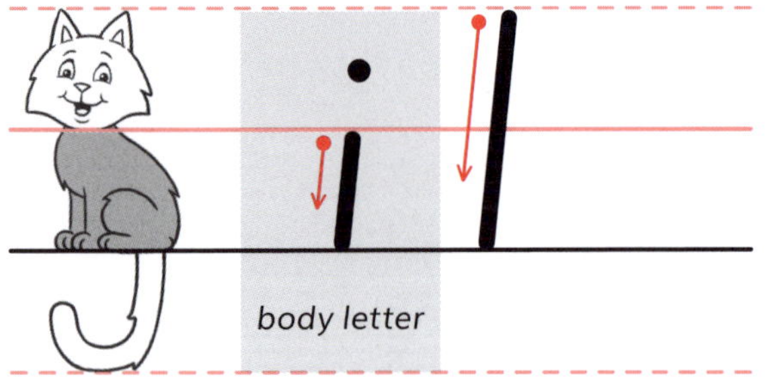

ice cream

Track.

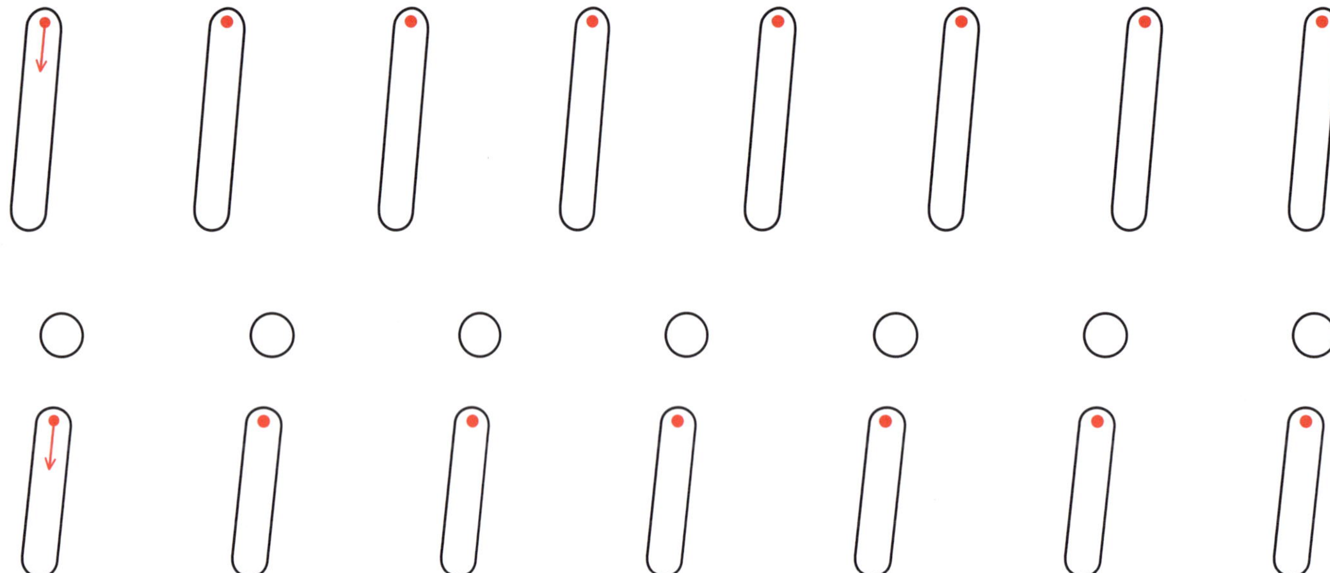

Find ‘i’.

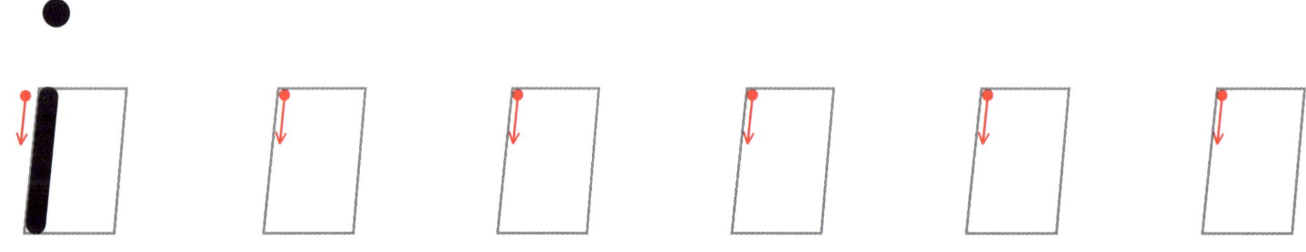

Trace and copy. Complete the lines.

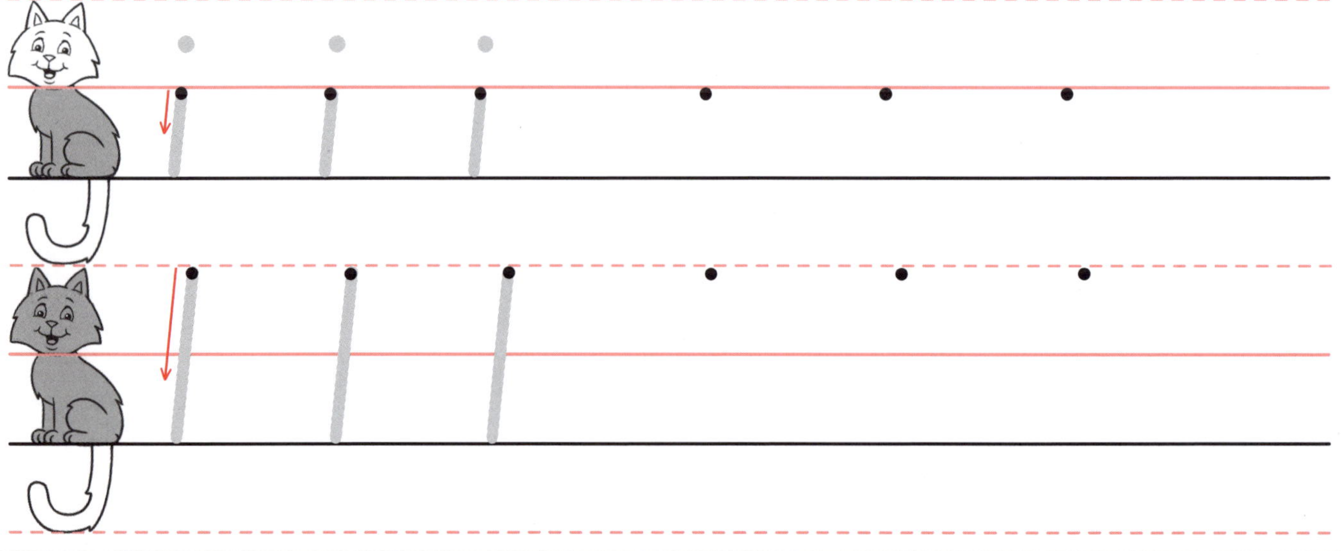

Trace and copy.

into into into into

"I will put some air

into your tyre."

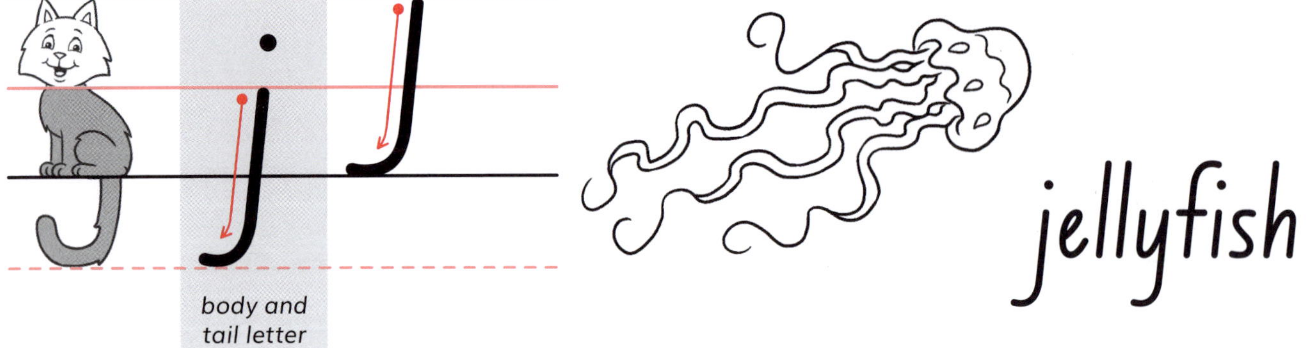

Track.

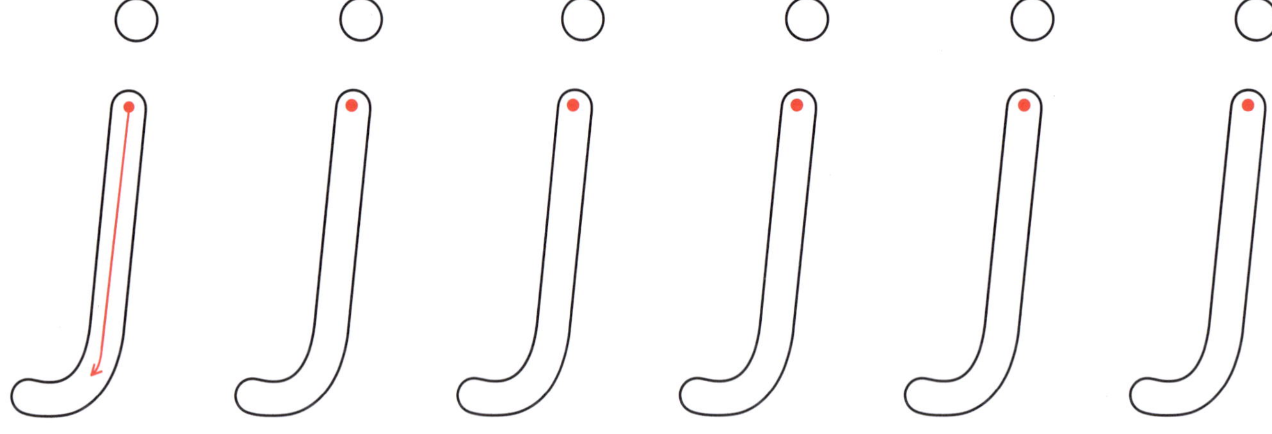

Find ‘j’.

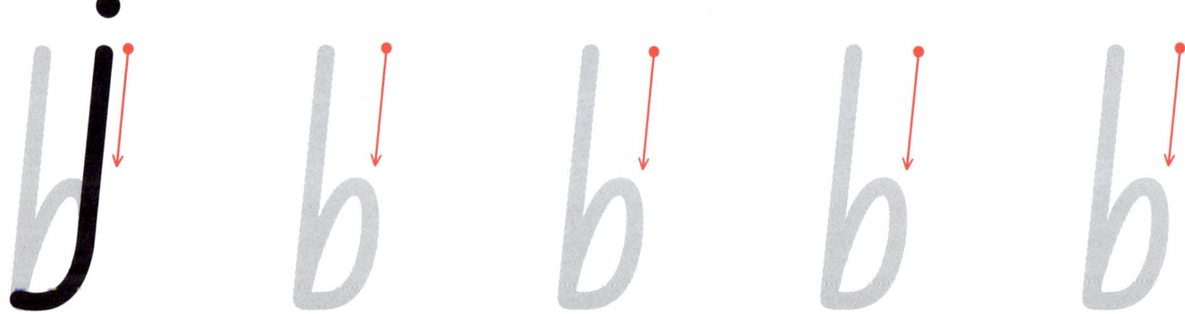

Trace and copy. Complete the lines.

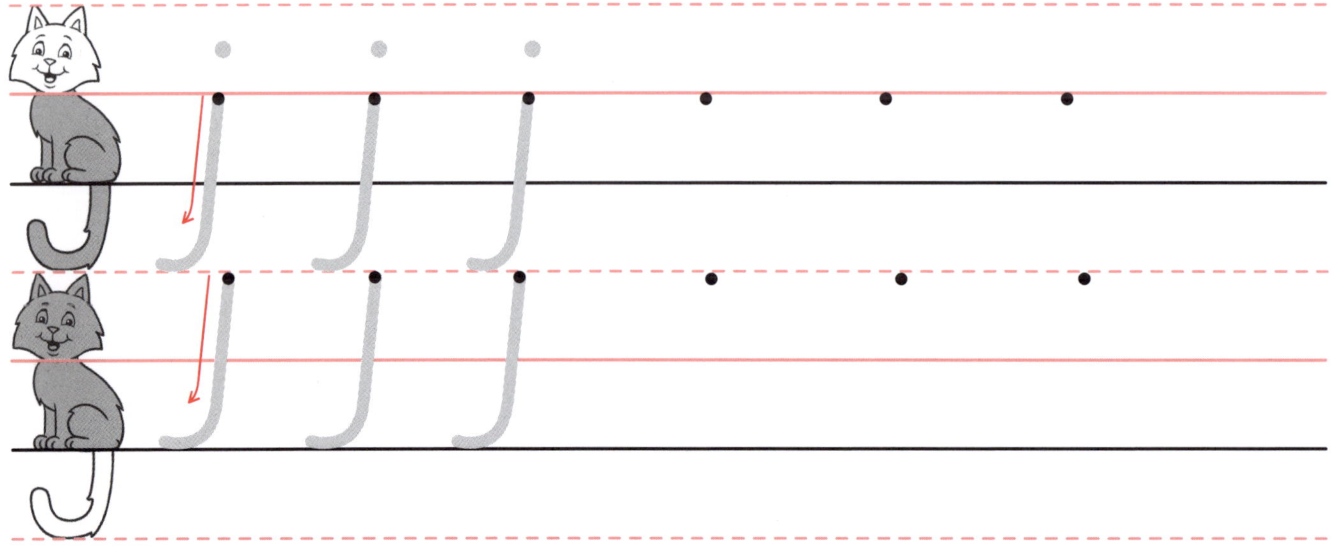

Trace and copy.

just just just

"You just have to

stay very still."

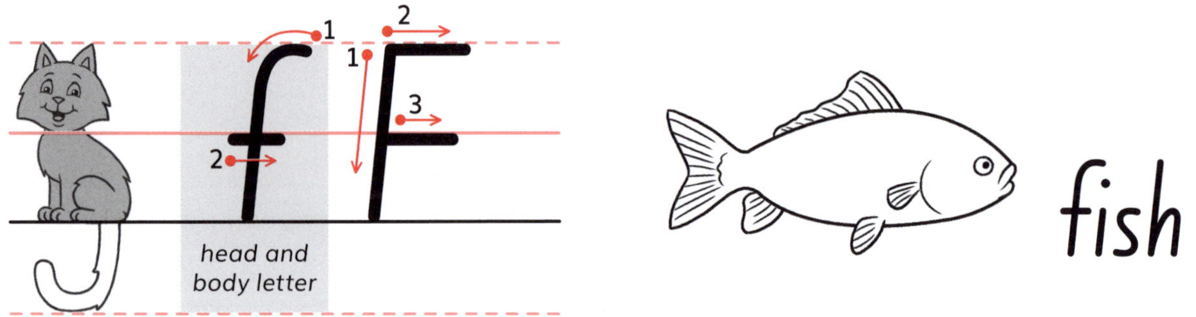

Track.

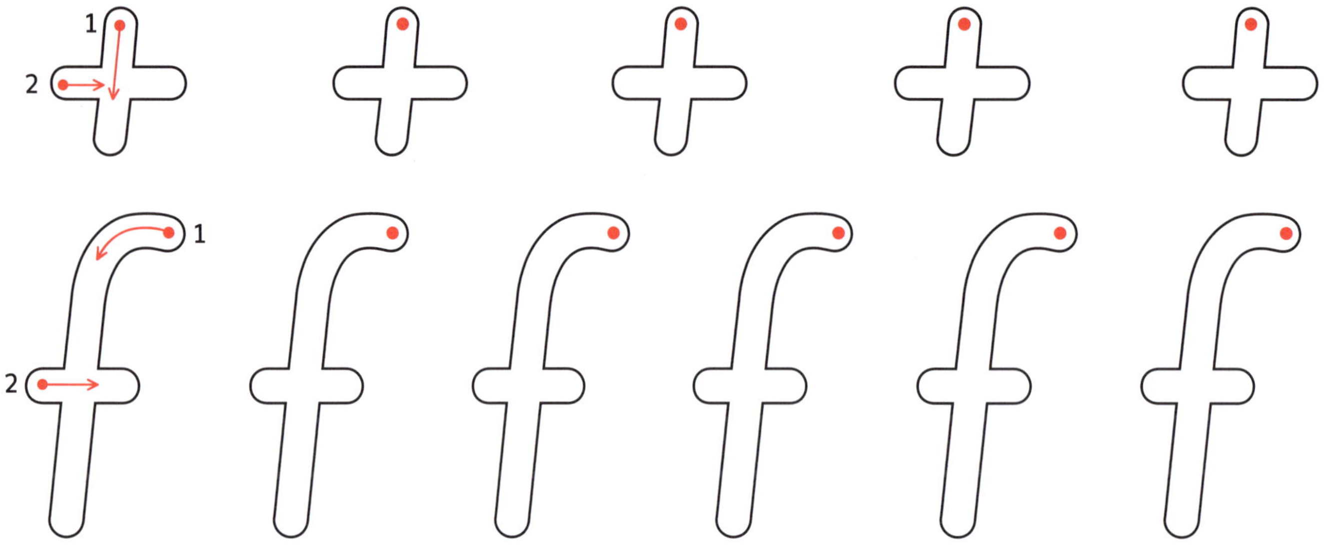

Find 'f'.

Trace and copy. Complete the lines.

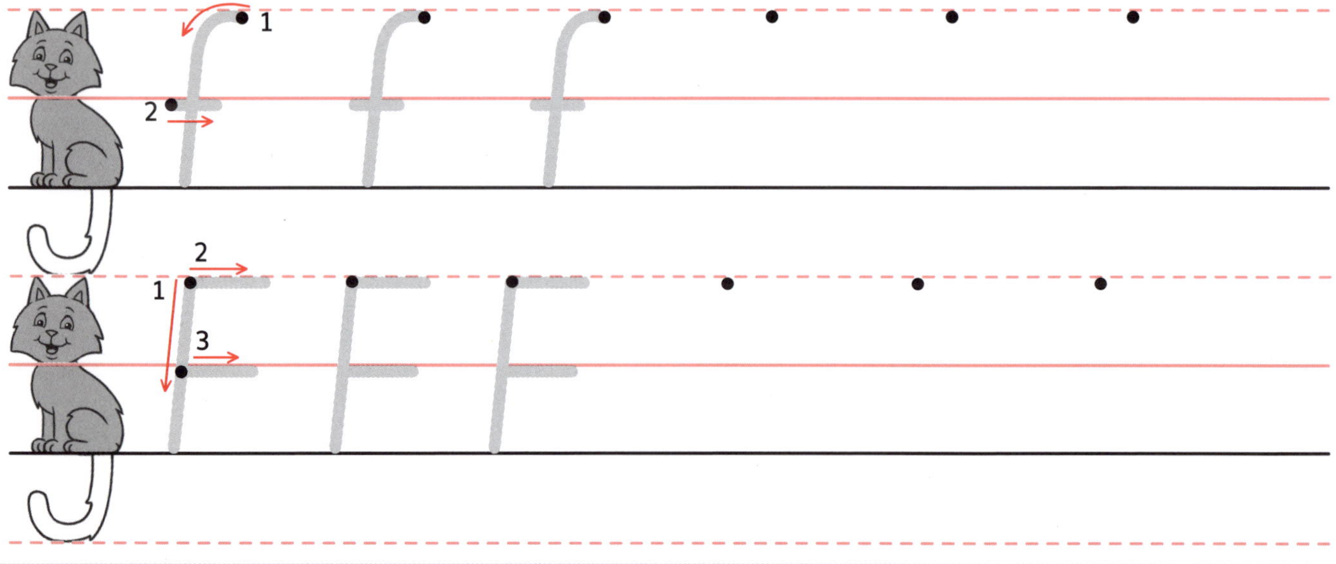

Trace and copy.

felt felt felt felt

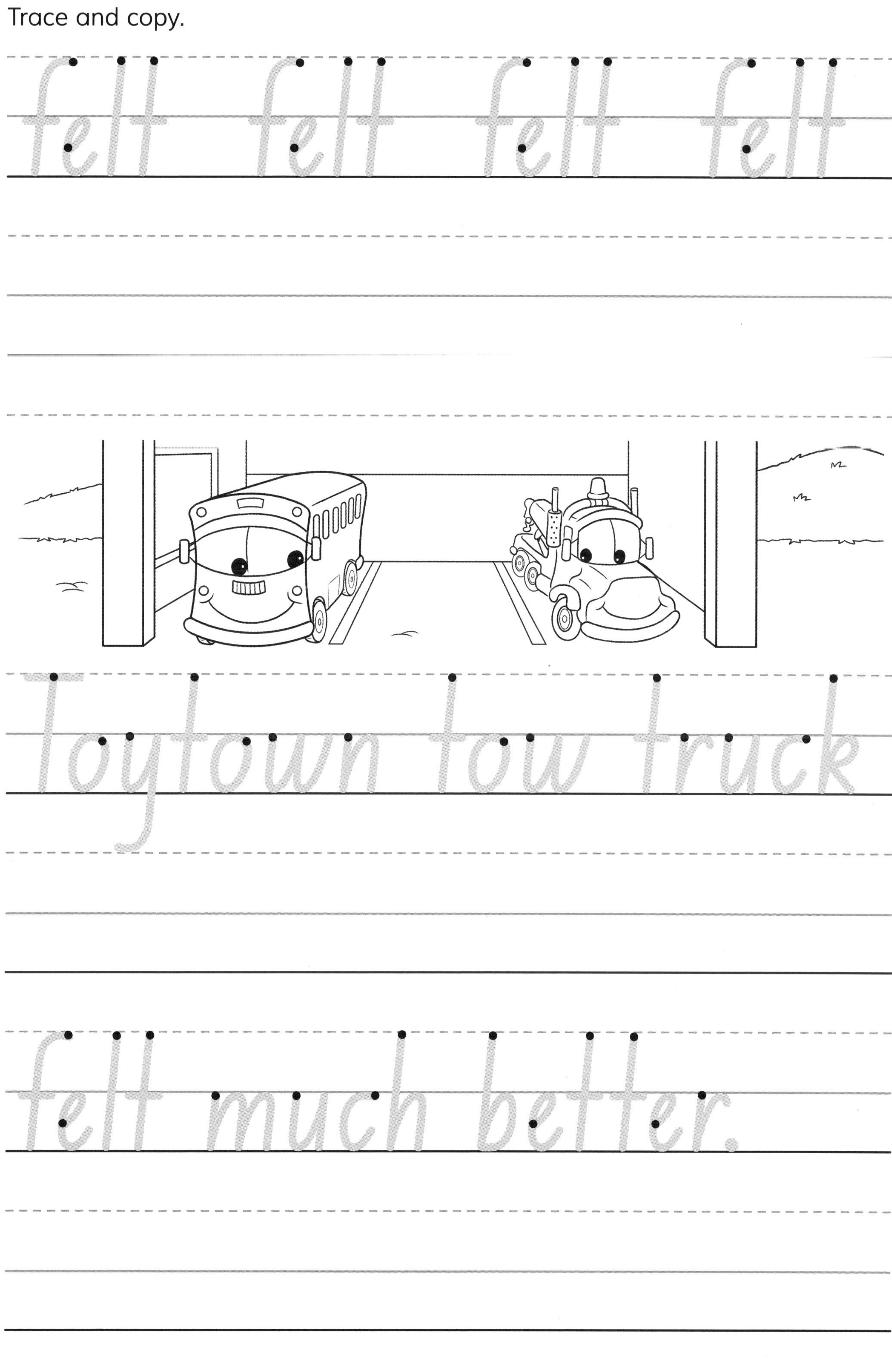

Toytown tow truck

felt much better.

Track.

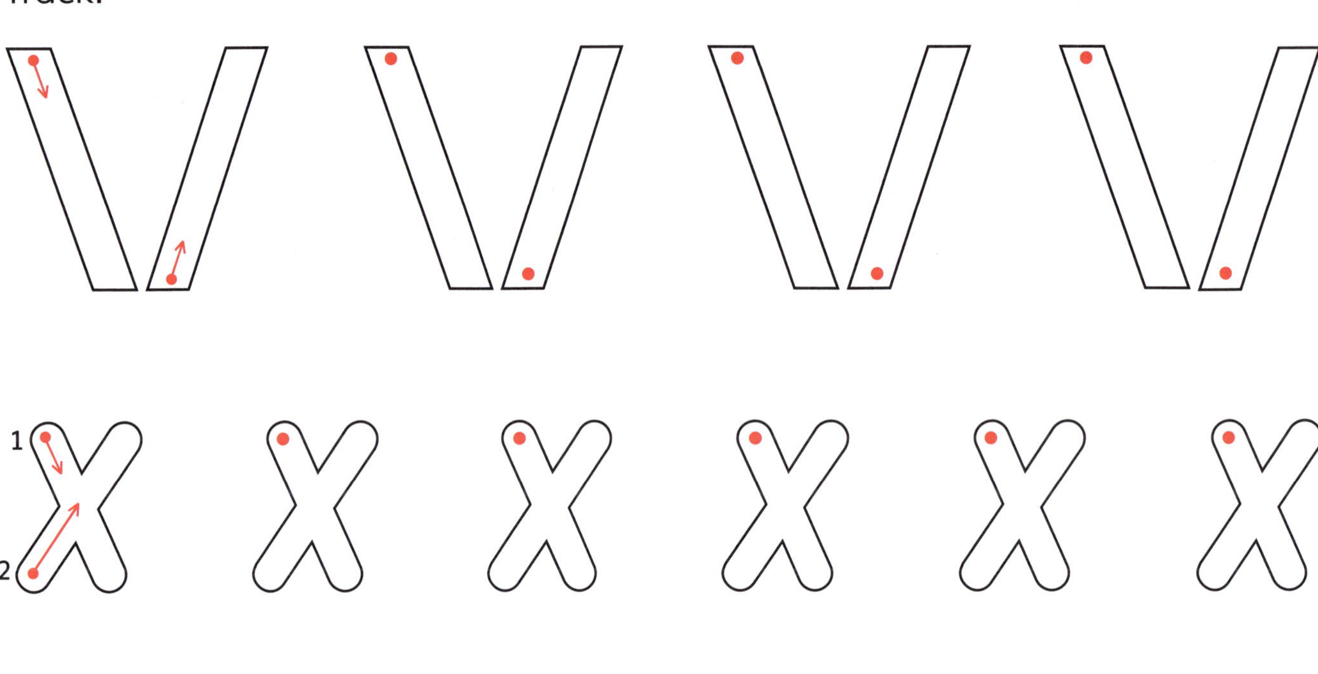

Find 'x'.

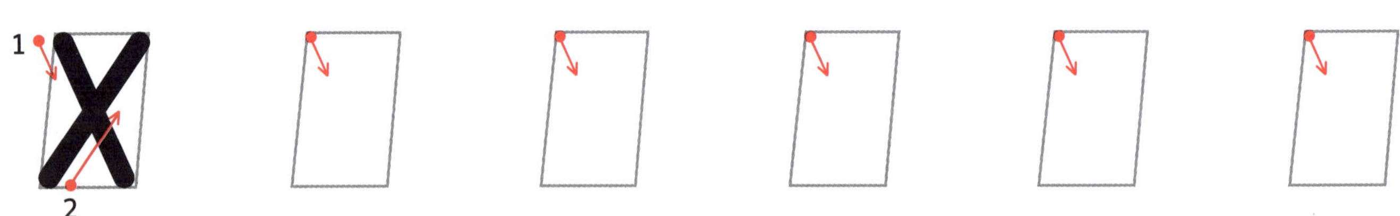

Trace and copy. Complete the lines.

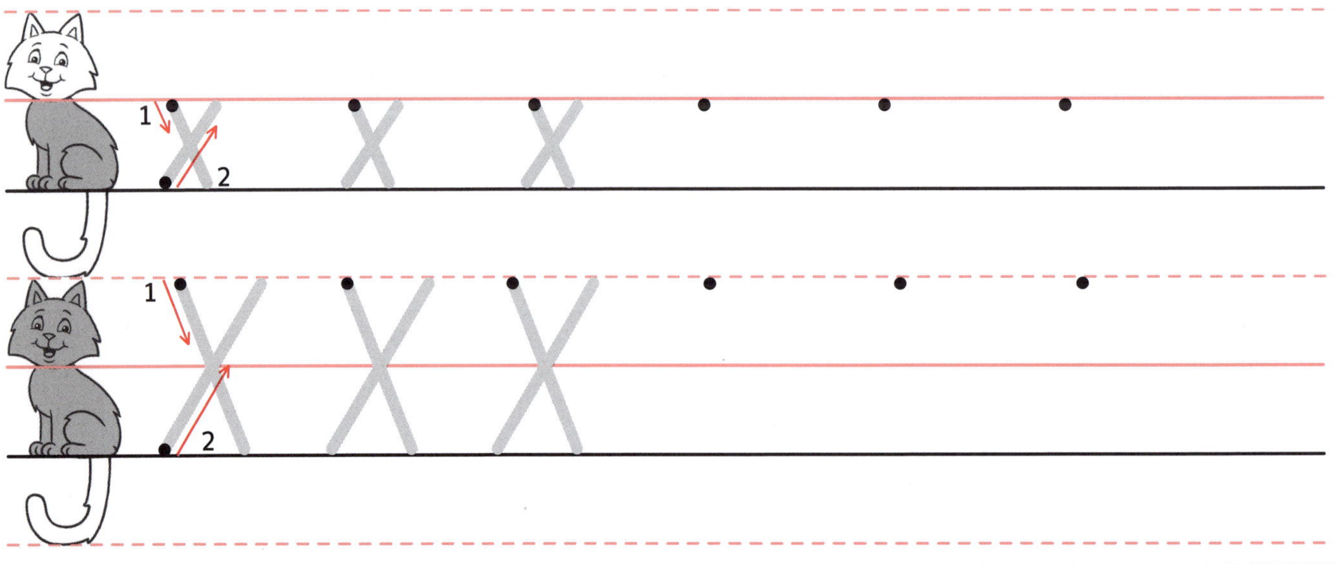

Trace and copy.

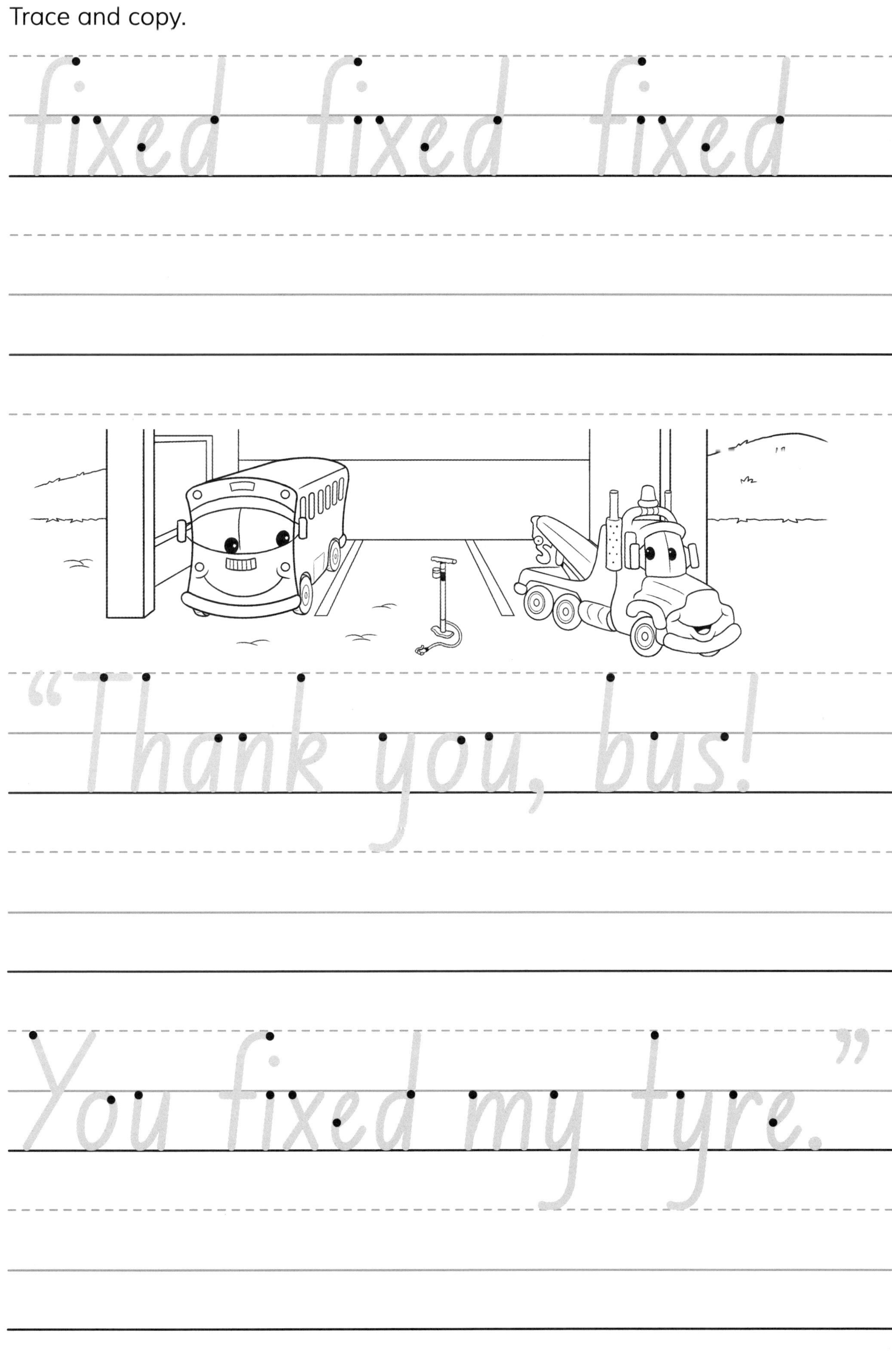

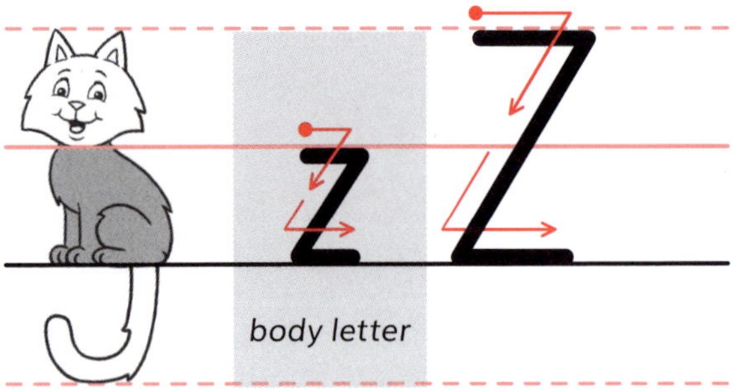

z Z

body letter

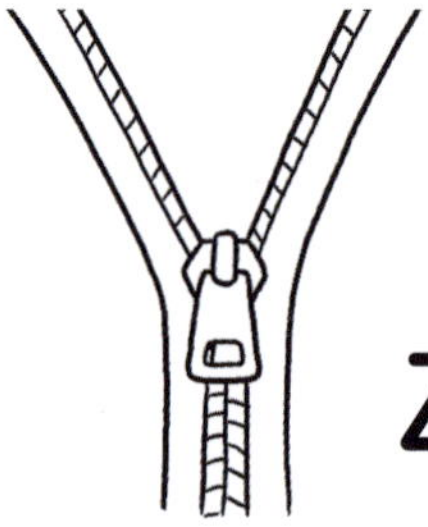

zip

Track.

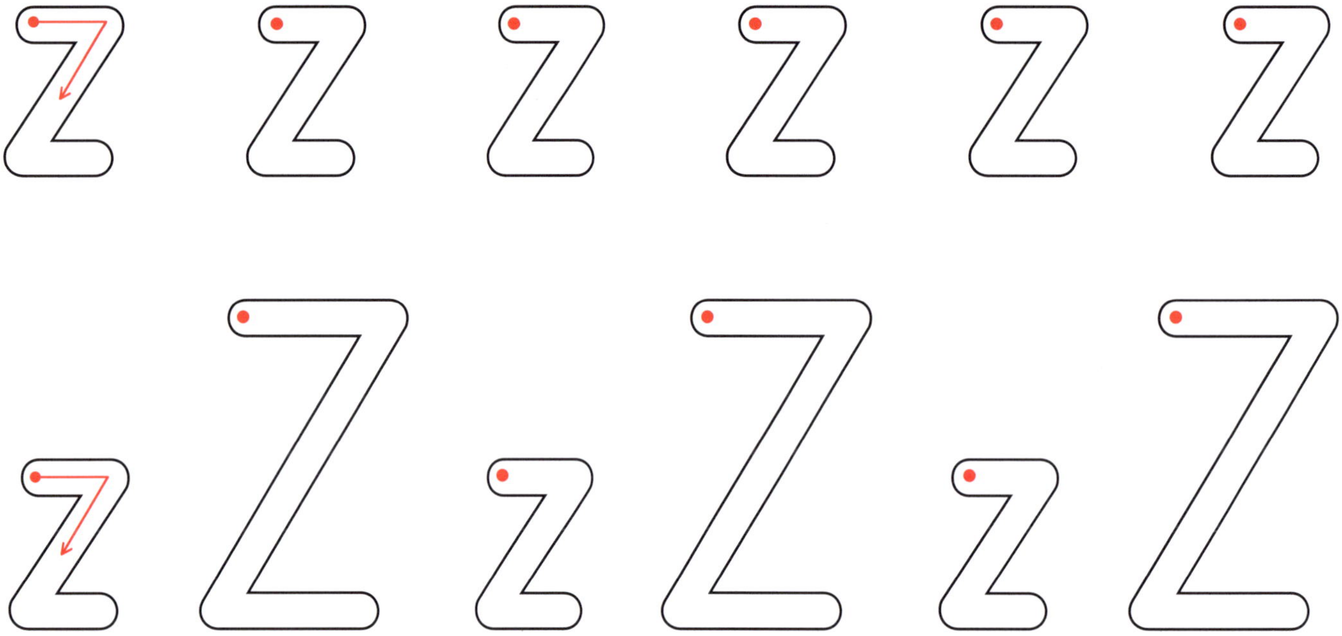

Find 'z'.

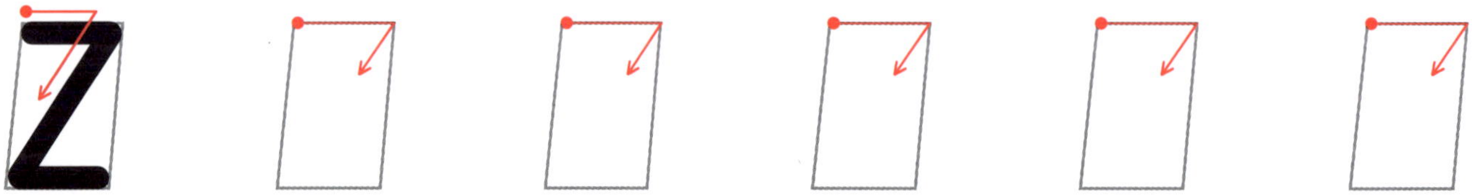

Trace and copy. Complete the lines.

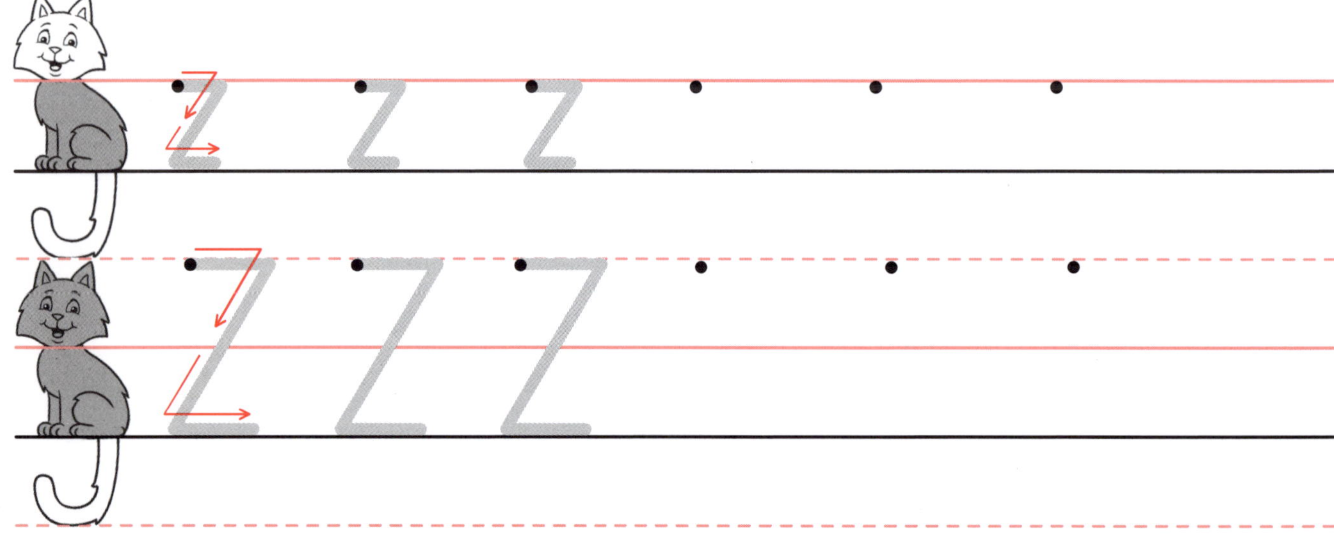

Trace and copy.

zoom zoom zoom

get.ga/PMWA65

Now the tow truck

could zoom away.

Trace and copy.

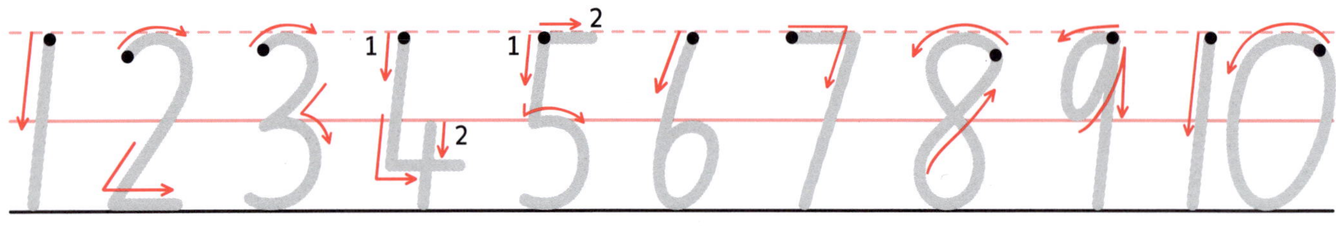

1 one 2 two

3 three 4 four

Trace and copy.

5 five 6 six

7 seven 8 eight

9 nine 10 ten

Trace.

20 twenty

30 thirty

40 forty

50 fifty

60 sixty

Trace.

70 seventy

80 eighty

90 ninety

100 one hundred

Teacher observation guide

Student is: left-handed ☐ right-handed ☐

Student demonstrates correct posture, paper position and pencil grip. ☐

Student is stroking from top to bottom. ☐

Student is stroking from left to right. ☐

Student is tracking accurately. ☐

Student is tracing accurately. ☐

Student follows simple verbal rehearsal to form letters. ☐

Student forms lower-case letters with accuracy:

a	b	c	d	e	f	g	h	i	j	k	l	m	n	o	p	q	r	s	t	u	v	w	x	y	z

Student forms capital letters with accuracy:

A	B	C	D	E	F	G	H	I	J	K	L	M	N	O	P	Q	R	S	T	U	V	W	X	Y	Z

Student can write the numerals 1–100. ☐

Student uses head, body and tail character to describe the spatial properties of letters. ☐

Student can identify wedges within a letter pattern. ☐

Student is placing letters correctly within lines. ☐

Student can copy a word with accuracy. ☐

Student can copy a complete sentence with accuracy. ☐

Notes:

....

....

Date: ....

CERTIFICATE

get.ga/PMWC7